BUDGET DEFICITS AND MACROECONOMIC POLICY

(

Budget Deficits and Macroeconomic Policy

J. O. N. Perkins
Emeritus Professor
University of Melbourne
Australia

First published in Great Britain 1997 by
MACMILLAN PRESS LTD
Houndmills, Basingstoke, Hampshire RG21 6XS and London
Companies and representatives throughout the world

A catalogue record for this book is available from the British Library.

ISBN 0–333–65660–1

First published in the United States of America 1997 by
ST. MARTIN'S PRESS, INC.,
Scholarly and Reference Division,
175 Fifth Avenue, New York, N.Y. 10010

ISBN 0–312–17553–1

Library of Congress Cataloging-in-Publication Data
Perkins, J. O. N. (James Oliver Newton), 1924–
Budget deficits and macroeconomic policy / J.O.N. Perkins.
p.   cm.
Includes bibliographical references and index.
ISBN 0–312–17553–1 (cloth)
1. Budget deficits.   2. Macroeconomics.   3. Economic policy.
I. Title.
HJ2005.P47 1997
339.5'23—dc21   97–7102
                                                               CIP

This book is printed on paper suitable for recycling and made from fully managed and sustained forest sources.

10   9   8   7   6   5   4   3   2   1
06   05   04   03   02   01   00   99   98   97

Printed in Great Britain by
The Ipswich Book Company Ltd
Ipswich, Suffolk

To the memory of Kirker Stephens of the University of Oklahoma at Norman – who took the trouble to let me know that there was at least one other economist in the world who realised the importance of an appropriate mix of monetary measures, government outlays and taxation in achieving macroeconomic objectives – in the hope that he would have approved of this development of our ideas.

Contents

List of Tables

Preface

This book develops and builds upon the analysis of earlier books (1979, 1982, 1985, and 1990), in which I discussed the importance of thinking of macroeconomic policy in terms of the level of government outlays, the level of taxation and the setting of monetary policy as being at least three instruments (and not merely in terms of the two instruments, 'fiscal' and 'monetary' policy).

The basic rationale for this approach is that different macroeconomic instruments have different effects on inflation, and also on the current account balance or the change in national net wealth, for the same effect on real GDP. The effects of the different instruments on these other objectives were in those books related to ('standardised by') the effect of each broad category of policy upon real GDP. Empirical work used to illustrate the arguments relied largely upon simulations for the UK and for the seven major OECD countries and the EEC (as it was in the mid-1980s).

The present work draws on a much wider range of simulations with macroeconomic models, including several for smaller countries, and one computable general equilibrium model (for the US). Several of these cover a number of different types of tax change and different types of government outlays. This makes it possible to illustrate the importance of disaggregating the fiscal instruments into several types of outlay and several types of tax.

The main difference from the earlier contributions is, however, that the effects of the various instruments are related to ('standardised by') their effects on the budget balance. The purpose of this is to illustrate that changes in the budget balance ('reducing the budget deficit') are not a useful indicator of either the setting of policy or the direction of the effects of changes in macroeconomic policy upon any of the macroeconomic objectives. For that would be so only if the various fiscal instruments had the same effect on a given macroeconomic objective (output, employment, inflation and so on) for the same effect on the budget balance. As the empirical evidence drawn upon here (as well as a priori arguments) indicate, this does not appear to be true. Discussions of fiscal policy changes in terms of their effect on the budget balance are thus as likely as not to give dangerously misleading indications of the effects of those policy changes.

The general reader may prefer to omit the detailed analysis of simulations in Chapters 3 to 7, a summary of which is contained in Chapter 8. The main analysis, argument and conclusions may be found in Chapters 1, 2 and 9.

I am indebted to Duncan Ironmonger, Joe Isaac, John Nevile, Kim Sawyer and Jack Sullivan for their comments on earlier drafts. None of these bears any responsibility for remaining deficiencies.

J. O. N. Perkins, Melbourne, August 1996

1 Introduction

A great deal of discussion of macroeconomic policy in most countries recently has been expressed in terms of changes in the level of the budget deficit. Attention in the USA has been focused on the alleged need to bring down the budget deficit, and even to 'balance the budget'. One of the principal criteria for entry into the proposed European Monetary Union is that a member should have a budget deficit no higher than a certain target ratio to its GDP, and keep it there, as well as holding down the existing level of its national debt to a certain ratio to GDP. In Britain, discussions of fiscal policy are generally centred around the target of a certain figure for the Public Sector Borrowing Requirement or 'PSBR'. More recently attention seems to have been given primarily to the level of the PSBR in excess of government investment. (Less commonly, in order to avoid the erroneous though widespread practice of taking the sale of public sector assets as a budget credit, the term Public Sector Financing Requirement or 'PSFR' is sometimes used in Britain.)

But this 'intermediate target' of the level or direction and size of changes in the budget deficit (or the PSBR) as an intermediate target for policy is potentially highly misleading as an indication of either the existing setting of fiscal policy or of the direction and extent to which fiscal policy ought to be changed. This is not to say that government borrowing (the budget deficit) is without social costs. In particular, the taxation needed to service extra debt inflicts real costs on the economy in future periods. But the budget deficit is itself merely the result of the different forms of government outlays and revenue. It therefore makes no sense to talk of reducing the budget deficit without discussing also the particular combinations of measures, on the outlay or revenue side (or both), by which that change is to be brought about. Only by stating what changes on either or both sides of the budget are being advocated can any useful policy discussion take place; for all the various possible combinations of changes in different government outlays and receipts are likely to have different effects on any or all of the fundamental objectives of macroeconomic policy.

They will of course also have different social and economic effects of other sorts – on the allocation of resources and the distribution of income, in particular; but these are generally the subject of widespread discussion, and are usually taken into account as bases for government fiscal policy decisions. The discussion in this book, however, is devoted to the *macroeconomic*

1

consequences of various possible fiscal measures, to illustrate the point that changes in the budget balance, or its level, are not a useful guide to macroeconomic policy-making.

Analogy with Private Sector Borrowing

The criteria for determining the level of public sector borrowing are essentially similar to those that are taken into account when businesses and households are taking decisions about their level of borrowing.

Robert Eisner has put this point in a way that should make it convincing to everyone:

> I am fond of asking audiences how they feel about debt. Is it good or bad? A majority of hands indicates that debt is bad. Then I ask, 'how many of you borrowed to buy a house? Or how many of your parents did?' A sizable majority of hands rises in the affirmative. 'How many of you think that was bad?' No hands are raised and I follow up, 'Then you are not so sure that debt is generally bad!'
>
> (Robert Eisner, 'Deficits and Us and Our Grandchildren'
> in James M. Rock (ed.),1991, p. 81)

To speak of public sector borrowing as if it were in some sense always 'bad', and should therefore be reduced, is as absurd as suggesting that businesses or individuals should never borrow. But it is always true that a borrower can misuse borrowed funds, and so be in a position where it would have been better if the borrowing had never been undertaken. For a business, the broad principle is that the borrowing should be put to uses that enable it to increase its profits (by comparison with what they would otherwise have been) on a sufficient scale to service the borrowing – and still leave some additional profits for the business. Some households and individuals may also borrow for similar purposes – to increase their earning-power sufficiently to pay interest on the debt and eventually to repay it; though individuals may also borrow to see them through times of difficulty for themselves or their family, in order to sustain their consumption in the immediate future, in the expectation that their incomes will rise (for reasons not associated directly with the loan), or that their family commitments will fall over the period of the borrowing and its repayment. Such borrowing may or may not make possible an increase in the family's income over time; but, in any case, it may enable the family to spread its income and payments over time in a way that it expects to increase its welfare in the longer run.

In all these cases, there are risks that the borrowing will turn out to have been ill-judged. Borrowing always carries some costs. The relevant question is therefore always whether the game is worth the candle – whether the benefits that result indirectly from undertaking the borrowing will or will not exceed those inevitable costs.

Exactly the same is true of government borrowing. It always carries real (gross) social costs – but this is not a valid reason to speak of it as if it were inherently to be avoided (as often seems to be the implication of much public discussion of government borrowing). The relevant consideration is always whether the social benefits will or will not exceed the social costs. In other words, whether a *net* social benefit will result.

It should, however, be added that there are certain differences between government borrowing and that undertaken by businesses or households. In the first place, when governments decide how much, and in what form, they are going to increase their borrowing they may be looking to their short-term political advantage, and hoping that any costs their decisions may inflict on posterity will have to be borne by their successors. This may especially be a risk if they have reason to believe their political opponents will be in power when the costs of the borrowing become clear, while the benefits in the short-term may be to the political advantage of the government undertaking the borrowing. But in the last resort the ballot box is the way in which such decisions are judged in a democracy; and unwise political decisions are not inherently different in matters relating to government borrowing from any other decisions about policy.

Another difference between a government on the one hand and a private borrower on the other is that governments can if necessary create the money to pay their debts, whereas a business that fails to pay will eventually become bankrupt – and well before that happens it may have lost the confidence of investors, making it unable to borrow (except, perhaps, at prohibitive rates of interest). One reason why financial markets often look with disfavour on high levels of government borrowing is probably the fear that excessive borrowing by a government can lead it to resort to money creation to finance its debt or its servicing, or to permit a high rate of inflation in order to reduce the real burden of the debt it has created. If such fears arise (even if they are misplaced) their adverse effect on the government's credibility, and its ability to borrow, may have real social costs for the country.

There is also the point – more directly relevant to the analysis and discussion of macroeconomic policy in the present book – that the economic decisions of a government, including its borrowing, may affect the general level of activity, as well as inflation and the level of the community's net wealth, in ways that a government will normally try to take into account;

whereas no business (except, perhaps, a very large international conglomerate operating in a very small economy) can take account of the effects that its actions may have on the economy as a whole.

Yet these differences between governmental and private borrowing do not nullify the basic similarities: in both cases, the relevant borrowing decisions ought to be taken in the light not only of the amount of the borrowing and the cost of servicing it, but – equally – of the use to which the borrowed resources are to be put, and whether these benefits will exceed the costs involved. In the case of a government, some of the benefits may include ones that are not quantifiable in monetary terms, and ones that yield a return in non-financial forms. Most defence spending and most forms of spending on public amenities are of this nature. These do not normally add to the government's ability to service the debt. But, on the other hand, if the government's policy decisions, including those relating to its borrowing, result in a rise in total output, whether in the short term or the long term, the country's ability to sustain the extra governmental debt will normally be enhanced, even if it cannot be shown to have been used in ways that directly produce a return that can be used to service the debt. In this may lie another reason why financial markets are suspicious of high levels of government borrowing: for when the return takes such indirect and often unquantifiable forms, it is obviously especially difficult (or even impossible) to assess whether the extra borrowing will prove to be worth while.

One might argue that this almost inevitable suspicion of government borrowing in financial markets may lead governments to be unduly cautious about borrowing – though it may also act as a salutary restraint upon them.

OUTLINE OF REMAINING CHAPTERS

In the ensuing chapters, Chapter 2 discusses some general considerations relating to budget deficits; Chapter 3 considers the effects on output of alternative fiscal measures having the same effect on the budget balance; Chapter 4 discusses the likely effects on employment and unemployment of different sorts of government outlays and different sorts of taxation; and Chapter 5 the effects on inflation of different forms of taxes and government outlays. Chapter 6 discusses the ways in which different fiscal measures may affect net national wealth – the current account balance together with the proportion of output being devoted to productive investment. Chapter 7 discusses the relevance of the setting of monetary policy and of the exchange rate to determining the macroeconomic effects of different changes in government outlays and revenue. Chapter 8 outlines the ways in which different combinations of fiscal measures may be used to approximate to the best outcome for the country in terms of not only the costs of government borrowing, but also in terms of the effects on the various macroeconomic objectives. A concluding chapter considers some of the policy implications of the analysis, including the question of whether targeting the level of the budget deficit (or government borrowing) may have a salutary effect by way of making governments more responsible.

2 General Considerations

This chapter outlines some general considerations relating to the running of budget deficits. In particular, it discusses whether there are any general criteria that can usefully be applied to decisions about the level of government borrowing, and the budget deficit.

Rules of Thumb about Borrowing

The difficulties about foreseeing the effects of a given loan made to a government (which have been mentioned in Chapter 1) probably help to explain why simple rules of thumb are sometimes used to decide whether a government's debt or borrowing appears to be excessive. Thus among the criteria for entry into the European Monetary Union are the level of a government's budget deficit and its total level of debt relative to the country's total output. Enough has been said in Chapter 1 about assessing the costs and benefits of government borrowing to make it clear that any such ratios, plucked out of the air (so to speak), are the reverse of helpful in deciding whether a government's borrowing (or its budget deficit) is excessive or inadequate. For that will depend on the use made of the funds, and is likely to vary greatly from time to time and from one country to another.

It is often argued that if the rate of increase in a government's borrowing exceeds the rate of interest it has to pay on its borrowing, that is an unsustainable position; on the grounds that if this continued the debt would eventually rise without limit. It is true that if the total of the government's debt rises faster than the country's total output, that position is (ultimately) unsustainable, as the debt servicing would eventually come to exceed the whole of the country's output.

But these simple rules of thumb are not really defensible as a guide to whether a government should borrow more, or less, at the margin. For, irrespective of the existing level of the national debt, the borrowing should not be undertaken unless the country's total output (including whatever welfare benefits accrue from the spending of the borrowed funds) is expected to be increased sufficiently to service the debt. Any analysis in terms of the ratio of borrowing to total output sets aside these relevant considerations by assuming implicitly that the country's total output will not be increased by the borrowing (and the use made of those funds); whereas the relevant consideration is the effect of the borrowing on total output (including the

6

country's welfare generally) at the margin, compared with the costs of servicing the debt.

Similarly, the rate of increase in the debt relative to the rate of interest paid on it should not be considered in isolation from the use made of the funds; for the borrowing may or may not be worth while whatever the relationship between the rate of interest and the rate of growth of the debt.

In any event, to criticise borrowing on the grounds that *if* it continued at the same rate indefinitely it would become 'unsustainable' is not a valid criticism of borrowing that is *not* intended to continue indefinitely, and which can be used to facilitate the servicing of the loan and still leave the borrower better off than if the loan had not been raised.

Contributions to the literature that use as a guideline for borrowing the alleged need to keep the growth of borrowing to a lower rate than that of real output, are implicitly assuming that the extra borrowing will have no effect on the rate of growth of output (including the real social benefit of its welfare effects). But if that is true, there is in any event no case for the government borrowing, irrespective of the relationship between the growth of the national debt and that of national output. On the other hand, if – as ought to be true – the extra government borrowing will be used to change the rate of growth of the country's output, the relevant comparison is between the extra output that is thus made possible and the extra costs of servicing the national debt that are incurred as a result of the borrowing.

PROBLEMS OF DEFINITION

It has been rightly said that there are an almost limitless number of defensible ways to define the budget deficit. This means that the deficit can rise on one definition at the same time as it is falling on another equally reasonable definition.

Before considering some of the reasonable definitions, let us first consider one that is indefensible – at any rate as affording any guidance on macreconomic policy. This is the widely used definition of the budget balance that takes credit for the government's sale of public sector assets – as when nationalised industries are privatised. It is true that if the aim is to assess changes in the public sector's net (real) assets, its sales of existing real assets to the private sector (and any purchase of such existing real assets), can and should be brought into the account (though it will receive financial assets in return). Presumably this is the reason, or excuse, that would be offered for the otherwise extraordinary practice of counting the sale of public sector assets as negative government outlays in the context of the discussion of macroeconomic policy.

But from a macroeconomic point of view, the sale of public sector assets to private buyers cannot logically be considered as the opposite of public sector spending on the creation of new assets, which tends to increase output (at least in the industries in question, and probably over the economy as a whole); whereas the sale of existing public sector assets is certainly not a negative form of government spending from a macroeconomic point of view. In any discussion of macroeconomic policy, therefore, the relevant forms of government investment spending are those on the creation of new real capital (roads and schools, and so on). Purchases of existing assets by the public sector from the private sector (or vice versa) do not lead to any creation (or reduction) of incomes. When existing assets are transferred from one sector to the other, there is merely a re-allocation of existing assets between sectors, so that there is no reason to expect that such transactions will have any direct macroeconomic effect, unless the payment to the government for the privatisation of assets causes a reduction of liquidity in the private sector that leads to a reduction in private spending.

One pernicious consequence of looking at the sale of public sector assets as a way of reducing the budget deficit is that it may induce governments to sell assets in order to have this cosmetic effect on the budget – and thus appear to unsophisticated eyes as being more 'financially responsible' than in fact they are. It may also induce governments to sell the assets at less than their full market price in order to achieve the sale during the period for which they are drawing up their budget. Moreover, it may lead governments to give the assets they are privatisting a stronger, or more monopolistic, position than would be justified in the social interest, in order to make the assets more attractive to buyers. There are what appear to be examples of each of these undesirable effects in the privatisation programme of the British government in fairly recent years.

There is, however, a case for considering outlays on new capital goods separately from the government's current outlays, especially if one is concerned with the influence of government outlays upon the country's stock of capital goods. If the markets and public discussion focus on the total of all government outlays (on newly produced capital goods, plus that on current transactions, including transfer payments), pressure on governments to 'reduce the budget deficit/PSBR' will often lead to disproportionate reductions in government outlays on useful capital goods, as these forms of cuts are usually politically less sensitive than those on current transactions. But cuts in capital items tend to inflict most of the costs of these cuts on future generations – or at least, on future years – whereas one reasonable target for macroeconomic policy is to ensure that the country does not live off its capital in the sense of holding down unduly the stock of useful capital goods that it hands on to posterity. Any discussions of macroeconomic policy that are concerned with changes in the country's net wealth (in this sense) should therefore at least separate the budget into transactions involving the creation of real capital goods, on the one hand, and its current transactions (the purchase of goods and services together with its transfer payments – such as unemployment benefits and pensions) on the other.

But such a separation of current from capital transactions is very difficult to make in a way that is completely acceptable; for many of the government's payments that are recorded as current items may make important contributions to the country's stock of useful material and (especially) human capital. This is true of many educational expenditures, and much of the health budget. On the other hand, many expenditures in those categories are more appropriately regarded as current consumption. Some attempts have been made to allow for this by including some more or less arbitrary fraction of the total expenditure on health and education as part of the government's capital outlays. But it seems unlikely that a completely acceptable way of doing this will ever be devised.

The budget deficit as usually defined fails to make allowance for the extent to which the government is failing to allow appropriately for depreciation on its real assets. So far as it is failing to do so, the net real assets of the public sector (and, indeed, of the country) are being allowed to fall; net real expenditure by the public sector (and the country as a whole) thus being lower at any given nominal level of investment than if the real value of the public sector assets was being adequately maintained.

Another item that is not usually accounted for in budgetary accounts is the future liabilities of the government for pensions and similar payments. These liabilities accrue for the most part well in advance of the time when they will have to be paid out; and a full accounting of public sector assets and liabilities should logically include an appropriate allowance for them as notional outlays. Some government obligations, notably guarantees of particular loans, are somewhat similar in nature, but even more difficult to account for as it is not known whether the guarantees will ever be called upon. Logically, one would like to be able to weight each of these liabilities by some index of the likelihood of their being drawn upon. On the other hand (as Duncan Ironmonger and John Nevile have both pointed out to me), if one is going to take account of the present value of the future costs to a government of the pension liabilities it is accruing, it would be logical also to take account, if some acceptable estimate of these could be made, of the present value of the future taxation capacity available to finance those future liabilities. (The difficulty of doing this may account for the neglect of this offsetting factor.)

Even apart from these difficulties of definition relating to items in the budget, there are other problems in deciding what sectors of the government, or of the public sector as a whole, should be covered in the definition that is being used. Generally macroeconomic policy is discussed in terms of changes in the fiscal policy of the central government of the country. But expenditures by sub-units, such as states, provinces, or local government areas are also important in assessing macroeconomic effects, so that the definition used should be one that includes only the net operations of the whole government sector – and not those transfers from a central government to smaller units of government that are not spent.

Statistics of the so-called 'general' government sector (which include these various sub-units of government as well as the central government) relate to this more macroeconomically relevant magnitude. But when the central government merely hands out funds to a sub-unit of government, this is usually counted in the central government's budget (and therefore as contributing to its budget deficit), whereas it is only when the sub-unit receiving the funds actually spends them that these funds have macroeconomic effects. (There is thus a close analogy between these funds and those transfers made to individuals – which also have their macreoconomic effects only when the recipients spend them.)

It is also possible for governments to have cosmetic effects on their own budget balances by reducing the extent to which they finance the deficits of nationalised industries, without this necessarily having any macroeconomic effects. If the government continues to subsidise a publicly owned corporation when it is transferred out of the budget, that does not, of course, reduce the budget deficit. But if the transactions that are now conducted 'off-budget' by the publicly owned corporation are now financed by that corporation borrowing from the public, whereas the same transaction would previously have been financed by government borrowing from the public, there are clearly no real macroeconomic effects resulting from the change. All that has happened is, so to speak, a 'change of name on the notepaper'. Such a reduction in the budget deficit is thus, from a macroeconomic point of view, purely cosmetic. A further danger in making a budget deficit into a policy target is thus that this may lead governments to shift some transactions 'off-budget'. Whatever the other costs and benefits of doing this, it is one further risk involved in allowing the budget deficit to become a target of policy.

Governments may also alter the timing of certain expenditures and receipts, in such a way that they incur them within one financial year rather than another, without this being of significance from a macroeconomic point of view – as the total payments and receipts reckoned over a slightly longer period than the financial year (say, thirteen instead of twelve months) at a monthly rate would be unaltered.

Effects of Inflation

One of the effects of inflation is to reduce the real value of all debts and assets that are expressed in monetary terms. Governments usually have large net liabilities in these forms; so that inflation tends to make their net asset position stronger, and to weaken that of people who own the bonds or other fixed-interest claims on the government. In this sense, inflation acts on the government's net debtor position in such a way as to reduce the real value of its net outstanding liabilities, much as would occur if it had raised taxes, thereby running a budget surplus, and used the proceeds to repay some of its debt. Various attempts have been made to assess the extent to which the nominal budget figures ought to be adjusted to allow for this factor; but the necessary adjustment has obviously become less important quantitatively than it was when inflation was higher. But even with inflation as low as 2% per annum, and taking by way of illustration two of the Maastricht criteria for entry to the European Monetary Union – a national debt of no more than 60% of GDP and a budget deficit of no more than 3% of GDP – a country on the verge of qualifying on the first of these criteria, but with a nominal budget deficit of 4% of its GDP would in fact be running a real budget deficit of less than 3% of GDP, (the inflation adjustment being 1.2% (that is, 2% of 60%) of GDP).

On the other hand, as the net liabilities of most governments continue to rise progressively, the stock of debt on which the inflation adjustment would need to be made has continued to rise. It is worth remembering, however, that so long as there is any inflation at all, and governments are substantial net debtors in terms of money-denominated financial assets, increases in the real value of the national debt and the real budget deficit (and increases in it) are always less than they are in nominal terms.

Cyclical Adjustment

In order to try to assess the effects of (discretionary) government budgetary decisions upon the economy, various attempts have been made to discount for the influence of the economy on the budget. For when the budget deficit falls as revenue rises (or unemployment benefits fall) as a result of its being a period of high activity, it is not appropriate to think of this as a tightening of fiscal policy in the discretionary sense. One body that makes regular estimates of changes in the so-called 'structural' budget balance (or 'cyclically adjusted' balance, as it might better be called) is the Organisation for Economic Co-operation and Development (the OECD). The International Monetary Fund also does so (for a range of individual countries); and so, more recently, does the secretariat of the European Union.

The choice of assumptions, especially about the target level of employment, on which such estimates are based is, however, to some considerable extent arbitrary. Such adjustments may therefore be made in a number of different ways, and will therefore give varying results as to whether, and if so how far, fiscal policy has been tightened. In any case, from the point of view of macroeconomic policy it may well be relevant to assess the effects not only of discretionary changes in taxation and government outlays, but also those that result from the responsiveness of revenue (and outlays) to rises and falls in activity. For in choosing their tax structure, governments have some discretion to decide how far to rely on these so-called 'built-in stabilisers' – especially progressive income taxation – to increase tax receipts sharply when activity rises and to reduce revenue more than proportionately when activity slows down; and, similarly, on the outlay side, so far as these are affected by the level of unemployment. If a government is aware of the operation of these automatic stabilisers, it may well consequently refrain from taking discretionary action that it would otherwise have deemed necessary. In order to assess the impact of fiscal policy as a whole, therefore, one may want to take account of the working of these automatic stabilisers. The changes in the structural (or 'cyclically adjusted') balance may then be thought of as indicative merely of *discretionary* changes made by a government in the period in question. It is probably more useful to look at cyclically adjusted figures as indicators of changes in fiscal policy; for the unadjusted figures including the built-in stabilisers give a false impression of the ease or tightness of fiscal policy. In particular, when the budget deficit rises in a recession it would be folly to take this as indicating an easing of fiscal policy – still more so to consider it to be an indication that fiscal policy needs tightening (the latter being an approach that one of Mrs Thatcher's ministers is reported to have well described as 'the economics of the madhouse').

This is an especially vivid example of the dangers of looking at changes in the actual budget balance as either an indication of what fiscal policy is doing (or trying to do), or of what it ought to be doing.

COMPARISON WITH OTHER FORMS OF TARGETING

There have in recent decades been waves of popularity for various forms of 'targeting' on particular economic magnitudes, especially (mainly in the 1970s) various monetary aggregates. These targets were usually not rigidly adhered to, and may have been used mainly as one form of guidepost to the thinking and policy decisions of central banks and governments. (One such monetary aggregate has continued to be an intermediate target in Germany.) In most countries, however, this fashion has passed; not only because of the difficulty of hitting such targets, but mainly because the relationship between any of these aggregates and the fundamental objectives of policy (low inflation and a high level of employment or growth) has turned out not to be at all close, and has varied with changing circumstances such as the deregulation of the financial system and various forms of financial innovation.

There was at one time – certainly in Britain – some confusion between the use of monetary aggregates as targets and the level of the Public Sector Borrowing Requirement. Milton Friedman (the most eminent advocate of monetary targeting) pointed to this confusion when giving evidence to a parliamentary committee in Britain. The basic point is that when a government runs a budget deficit (increases the PSBR) it may or may not finance it by creating money (or allowing the banks to create money). The alternative is for it to raise the finance by borrowing from the public. It is only the former method of financing that has implications for monetary growth.

For particular countries and in particular periods, efforts have been made to target the exchange rate or the rate of interest, or to reduce the level of government spending or tax revenue below a certain proportion of Gross Domestic Product. But none of these targets (especially when two or more of them have been targeted simultaneously) has proved to be closely related to the main objectives of economic policy. It is true that there have been periods when there has appeared to be such a relationship; but the mere fact that the authorities are known to be targeting such intermediate magnitudes appears often to have reduced the efficacy of that policy. For when people come to expect policy to react in a certain way they may act differently from the way in which they would have acted if they had had no such expectation. In particular, if the central bank is known to be targeting a monetary aggregate, this may lead both borrowers and financial intermediaries to change the form of their borrowing in such a way as to circumvent what would otherwise have been the effects on their actions of the official measures taken to reduce that aggregate. Borrowing through non-bank intermediaries tends then to be expanded relative to borrowing from banks. In the United States this combination of difficulties is usually thought of as one form of 'the Lucas critique', after the work of Professor Robert Lucas. In Britain (and a number of other countries) it is more usually thought of as 'Goodhart's law', after Professor Charles Goodhart, formerly of the Bank of England – especially when applied to the targeting of monetary aggregates, and when undue emphasis is placed on targeting that particular aggregate.

In any event, the unhappy experience that most countries have had in trying to achieve macroeconomic objectives by focusing on such intermediate magnitudes and the rate of growth of particular monetary aggregates, or the rate of interest, or the exchange rate, might reasonably have been expected to suggest caution about trying to use for that purpose another such target in the shape of the budget deficit or PSBR (on whatever definition). The fundamental reason for avoiding such targeting is that any such intermediate magnitude has only a very tenuous relationship to any one of the macroeconomic objectives; and any such relationship as there may be varies considerably from time to time and place to place – partly (though not wholly) as a result of its use for such purposes. Moreover, even when some such intermediate ('target') variable may seem to have some sort of relationship to a macroeconomic target (such as the rate of inflation) it is highly unlikely to be a good proxy for the complex combination of macroeconomic objectives (inflation, growth or employment, and perhaps the current account of the balance of payments or net national wealth) that governments have in mind. The search for such intermediate targets is a search for simpler ways of conducting macroeconomic policy with several objectives. Unfortunately, there is no such short cut. The setting of all the existing instruments of macroeconomic policy must be decided in the light of the best combination of them to achieve the best available approximation to all the economic objectives.

Disillusionment with such intermediate targets has led some commentators to suggest making the growth of nominal GDP the target of macroeconomic policy. This is probably preferable to any of the intermediate targets (including those relating to the budget balance). But its deficiency is that it implicitly assumes that inflation is unaffected by the combination of measures used to approximate the target rate of growth of nominal GDP. In fact, however, the choice of measures (the setting of monetary policy, of different government outlays, and of different forms of taxation) can have considerable effect upon the 'split' between real growth and inflation of any given nominal growth of GDP. This approach is therefore not an alternative to trying to choose the best combination of all the available instruments for achieving the best possible approximation to all the macroeconomic objectives.

3   Effects on Real Output

It would facilitate the setting of macroeconomic policy if one could generalise about the relative effects of each of the broad macroeconomic instruments on each macroeconomic objective. In the present context, it would be convenient to be able to say, for example, that government outlays generally have a more inflationary effect (at any rate for a given stimulus to real output or employment) than do tax cuts with the same effect on the budget balance; or that government outlays have a bigger upward effect on real output than a tax cut having the same effect on the budget balance.

This and the following chapters will analyse some of the reasons and evidence relating to why such generalisations cannot usually safely be made: for it depends largely on what types of government outlays are increased and what taxes are cut. But it facilitates the exposition to consider first the implications if it were true that government outlays in general and taxation in general can usefully be compared in terms of their effect on some macroeconomic objective for a given effect on the budget balance. Although this simple comparison is not sufficient, the analysis can then be applied also to a more useful comparison of the effects of particular government outlays with those of particular types of tax cut.

It will therefore be assumed for the purpose of this initial exposition that government outlays (or the particular government outlay in question) have a greater upward effect on real output than does a tax cut having the same effect on the budget deficit. The analysis can of course be readily applied to the opposite case with the obvious changes in wording.

The importance of such analysis is that only if all government outlays and all forms of tax cut having a given effect on the budget deficit have the same effect on the macroeconomic objective one is considering would it be useful to think of a change in the budget deficit as having some specific effect (in direction or size of effect) on the rate of growth of output, or employment, or the rate of inflation, as the case may be. In all other cases it is essential to analyse the effects on the macroeconomic objectives of alternative ways of bringing about a rise in the budget deficit of a given amount.

Take first the simplest case where one fiscal instrument – here assumed for the sake of argument to be government outlays (or one specific form of government outlay) – has a greater upward effect on real output than a tax cut having the same effect on the budget deficit. If the government wishes to hold down its rate of borrowing, and therefore the level of the budget deficit, but to provide a stimulus to output, it would do so by way of an increase in the relevant government outlays, rather than by way of tax cuts. Indeed, it would then – if an upward effect on real output were its only macroeconomic objective – be inclined to accompany the increase in government outlays by some rise in taxation. If these two increases were of the same size, under the present assumption this would constitute a balanced budget stimulus. Indeed, there would be some combinations of tax increase and increases in government outlays that could be chosen that would then provide a real stimulus while simultaneously *reducing* the level of government borrowing.

More generally, provided that there are at least two fiscal instruments that have different effects on real output for a given effect on the budget deficit, there is always some combination of them that can deliver a stimulus accompanied by a movement of the budget in the direction of surplus; and other combinations of them that can bring about a contraction of real output or employment accompanied by a movement of the budget in the direction of (greater) deficit.

Readers may easily convince themselves of this by taking any assumption about differences in the relative effects on real output or employment of government outlays and taxation respectively, and working through the total effects on output of either raising or reducing both of them, in such a way as to keep the budget in balance; and then find alternative ways of giving a stimulus with a movement of the budget towards surplus, or one that reduces output by means of a movement of the budget balance towards deficit. (The next five paragraphs may be omitted if the reader has by now been convinced that a movement towards a greater budget deficit need not be expansionary, and that some ways of changing the budget balance towards surplus may provide a stimulus.)

To take a simple example, let us assume that one fiscal instrument – call it 'government spending' – has an upward effect on real output of 3% (and a fall of government spending a downward effect of 3%), whereas a tax cut having the same effect on the budget balance over the period being considered by the government will lead to an increase in output of no more than 2% (and that a tax increase of the same order would reduce output by 2%). If the government's aim is to raise real output while minimising the upward effect on the budget deficit it will clearly be better for it to increase its expenditure than to cut taxes.

If there is, then, a rise in government spending of 1 million currency units, raising output by 3%, and the government simultaneously increases taxation by anything more than 1 but less than 1.5 million it will be able to stimulate output while also reducing the budget deficit; for the increase in spending will raise output by 3%, and the tax increase will reduce output by something less than 3%. An example of such a fiscal change would be:

	Change in government outlays +1 m	Change in taxation +1.4 m	Both together
Effect on output	+3%	-2.8%	+0.2%
Effect on budget balance	-1 m	+1.4 m	+0.4 m

The important conclusion is that so long as there is some fiscal stimulus that will raise output by more than some other (for a given effect on the budget deficit), it will not be *necessary* to increase the budget deficit in order to provide a fiscal stimulus.

Furthermore, there will, on those assumptions, by the same token be some ways of moving the budget balance in the direction of deficit that will actually reduce output. This may be illustrated by reversing the direction of the policy changes given in the last example – for example, by assuming that government outlays are cut by 1 million (reducing output by 3%) and taxation reduced by 1.4 million (increasing output by 2.8%), which will cause the budget to move in the direction of deficit but output to be reduced.

We see, therefore, that if different fiscal measures have different effects on output or employment for a given effect on the budget deficit, the running of a (greater) budget deficit should not be equated with the provision of a fiscal stimulus: for a stimulus may be given in ways that reduce the budget deficit; and so long as some forms of stimulus have a greater effect on output than some other(s) for the same effect on the budget balance, this means that it is not correct to assume that a government has provided fiscal restraint merely because it has reduced the budget deficit.

An analogous simple argument will indicate that a movement of the budget in the direction of deficit is not necessarily inflationary. To take another simple example: assume that an increase of a million in government spending raises inflation (over the relevant period) by 3%, whereas a tax increase of the same size leads to a fall in inflation, or an increase in it of less than 2%. A government that wishes to keep inflation down will then be inclined to increase taxes and to hold government outlays down, for any given budget balance that it may aim at. It would, on those assumptions, be possible for the budget deficit to increase without inflationary effects, provided that taxes were cut by less than 1.5 million for a cut in government outlays of a million; for the cut in government outlays would reduce inflation by 3%, and the cut in taxation would increase it by less than 3%, while the budget was moving in the direction of (greater) deficit.

More generally, if the government is concerned to provide a fiscal stimulus with a minimum upward effect on inflation, it should be concerned to find out what form of fiscal stimulus will have the least inflationary effect for a given stimulus to real output. Suppose that tax cuts increase inflation by 2% for a stimulus to real output of 1%; and that government spending having the same effect on the budget balance will increase inflation over the relevant period by 3% for a stimulus of 1%. Then, clearly, so long as the aim is both to hold down inflation and to stimulate output, tax cuts will be the preferable form of stimulus, rather than a rise in government outlays. A balanced budget reduction (both taxes and government outlays being reduced by the same amount) would in this case stimulate output and provide a better combination of inflation and real output than would a balanced budget increase.

In this example we have assumed that outlays and tax revenue having a given effect on the budget balance have the same effect on real output, but that a tax cut has that effect with less upward effect on inflation than the rise in government outlays. So long as the government wishes to keep real output up while minimising inflation, it will therefore do best to effect any given reduction in the budget deficit by reducing government outlays rather than increasing taxes, even though in this example we have assumed that the two forms of fiscal stimulus have the same effect on real output.

But suppose government outlays are the fiscal stimulus with greater effect on real output and are also the *less* inflationary of the two forms of stimulus, there will then be a double argument for giving any desired stimulus by raising government outlays, rather than by cutting taxes.

On the other hand, if the more expansionary of the two (for a given effect on the budget deficit) is the more inflationary for a given real stimulus, the government will have to take into account the relative effects on the budget balance (if it is concerned to keep this down) as well as the relative effects of the two instruments on inflation for a given real stimulus. If it is more concerned to hold down inflation (while providing a stimulus) it may then reasonably provide the stimulus in the least inflationary way, even if this involves a bigger rise (or smaller fall) in the budget deficit. More generally, however, if it is more or less equally concerned both with the effect on the budget balance and with the relative inflationary effects of the two instruments, its decision can reasonably be based on the extent to which instrument A (say, government spending) is superior to instrument B (say, tax cuts) from the viewpoint of holding down inflation, compared with the relative superiority of instrument B over instrument A from the viewpoint of holding down the budget deficit while providing a given stimulus.

A still greater complication will be that the government may attach different weights to the importance of holding down the budget deficit, on the one hand, and to holding down inflation (for a given real stimulus) on the other. Its decision will then need to be weighted by those preferences as well as by the expected relative superiority of each instrument in holding down the budget deficit, on the one hand, and holding down inflation (for a given real stimulus) on the other.

Of course, if the government is not concerned to stimulate output, but, rather, to hold down the level of demand in a period of high activity, similar principles can be applied in reverse. Given the assumption that government outlays have a bigger effect on output than a change in revenue of the same order, restraint applied through cuts in government outlays will have a bigger effect than tax increases in restraining demand for a given effect on the budget balance.

It should again be emphasised that under these assumptions it is not necessary to move the budget in the direction of surplus in order to restrain demand. But if the government wishes to reduce the budget deficit at the same time as restraining demand, it would in this case do best to cut its outlays more than it increases taxes, in the process of providing the fiscal restraint.

Given the same assumptions as in our first example, a reduction in government outlays of one million could be accompanied by a tax cut of more than one million but less than 1.5 million – which would clearly move the budget in the direction of deficit but still apply some fiscal restraint.

It must be added that the extent to which a government can apply these principles depends also upon its other policy objectives. There is always an upper (or lower) limit to be borne in mind about the extent to which any given element in the fiscal mix should be changed to achieve the objectives of high growth and low inflation. One of these may be termed the effect on 'net national wealth' – which includes changes in net debts owed to (or investment made in) the rest of the world (essentially the current account deficit or surplus), together with changes in the country's stock of productive capital. In addition, there are always considerations of income distribution and the allocation of resources that limit the extent to which governments can vary their fiscal instruments in the directions being suggested above.

OECD SIMULATIONS IN 1994

Some simulations for the OECD as a whole (published in 1994) are used by the authors to draw general conclusions about the relative effects of reducing government borrowing by a cut in government non-wage outlays or by certain combinations of tax increases. (Whether this evidence is sufficient to support general conclusions on this matter will be considered below.) The context of these simulations was to compare two different ways of reducing the budget deficits of the OECD by a stated amount over a period of years. Table 3.1 reverses the signs in this simulation, thus showing the estimated effects on real GDP of *increasing* the budget deficits of OECD countries progressively, either by increasing government outlays or by reducing a range of taxation (which was in fact direct taxation only – income tax and social security contributions), in such a way as to have the same effect on the budget deficit by each of those two methods in any given year, changing the budget deficit progressively over the period.

Table 3.1 shows that this simulation suggests that direct tax changes have a greater effect on both the level and rate of growth of real GDP on the average over a period of both three and five years than do government non-wage expenditures for the same effect on the budget deficit; and that by the third or the fifth year simulated the effect on the level of GDP is also greater for the package of direct taxation simulated than for an increase in government non-wage expenditure.

Table 3.1: *Simulated effects on real GDP of OECD of a rise in government non-wage expenditure and a cut in a range of direct taxes*
(Average %ge change in real GDP over five years, with change and levels in first three years in parentheses, for a 1% of GDP rise in government borrowing over the same periods)

	Government non-wage expenditures	Cuts in direct taxes
GDP growth rate	0.6 (0.7)	1.0 (1.3)
GDP levels	1.2 (1.3)	2.1 (2.1)
GDP growth rate in Year 5 (and Year 3)	0.5 (0.6)	0.9 (1.0)
GDP level in Year 5 (and Year 3)	1.2 (1.1)	2.1 (2.0)

The simulation used is that with unchanged real interest rates (an 'accommodating' monetary policy). The simulations in the original are for government non-wage expenditure *reductions* and for a range of direct tax *increases*: The signs have therefore been reversed in the table above.

The periods used are those beginning in the third year simulated, as no increase in government borrowing – or in the other magnitudes simulated – is assumed in this scenario for the first two years.

The policy changes simulated are for alternative means of having a given effect on the budget balance by the end of a stated period, with the 'slow-growth' scenario, and with a time-profile that maintains the same effect on the budget balance in each year for a change in government non-wage expenditures as for a change in a range of direct taxation in each year.

Source: Derived from Richardson et al. (1994).

The results shown in Table 3.2 are of another simulation for the whole OECD (also published in 1994) with a different pattern of expenditure and taxation changes over time. It also uses the OECD's Interlink model, but on this occasion assumes that monetary policy settings are such as to let the changes in fiscal policy have their natural effect upon real interest rates (a 'non-accommodating' monetary policy); so that when government outlays rise or taxes fall this increases real interest rates; and the effect this has on real output turns out to be great enough to lead, on balance, to a fall in real output over the first three years, especially as a result of increases in government non-wage expenditure.

Table 3.2: Simulated effects on growth rate of real GDP of OECD of changes in
government non-wage expenditures and direct taxation
(Five-year and three-year totals of %ge points change in rate of growth of real GDP for rise in government borrowing over the period equal to 1% of GDP, with effect in Year 3 and Year 5 in parentheses)

	Five-year	Three-year
Rise in government non-wage expenditures	0.13 (0.80)	–0.55 (0.00)
Cut in direct taxation	0.42 (0.67)	–0.40 (0.29)

The original simulation is for a *cut* in government non-wage expenditure and a *rise* in a package of direct taxation. The signs in the table above are therefore the opposite to those shown in the original source table. The years used are those beginning in the third year simulated, as no increase in government borrowing occurs in the first two years.

This simulation assumes that real interest rates are permitted to change as a result of the change in fiscal measures. The upward effect on real interest rates when government outlays rise or taxes are cut would lead to net 'crowding out' of other forms of expenditure in the first three years.

Source: Derived from Leibfritz et al. (1994).

But over the five-year period, cuts in direct taxation clearly have a greater effect in stimulating real GDP than do increases in government non-wage expenditures for a given effect on the budget deficit. (These results illustrate the important differences that may be made to the effects of fiscal instruments according to the period that is taken into consideration; and also that the particular assumption made about the setting of monetary policy is likely to have a bearing upon the size and direction of their effects – though not necessarily their ranking, which is a matter to be discussed in Chapter 7.)

Appraisal of These Results

Before one can draw general conclusions from the OECD simulations summarised in Tables 3.1 and 3.2 about alternative ways of reducing a budget deficit, one should bear in mind two special features of these simulations.

In the first place, the outlay side of the simulations relates only to government *non-wage* expenditures. We therefore cannot draw from these simulations conclusions about total government outlays (including government expenditure on wages and salaries). The results would thus apply to government purchases of goods, and such services as energy.

In the second place, we are told that the tax changes simulated relate to a range of different types of tax increase, without being told what pattern of tax increases is used. It is understood from the authors that it is a range of *direct* taxation – income tax and social security contributions – that is being simulated. Presumably the relative importance of the principal tax changes assumed in the simulations is similar to the proportions of these various taxes for the OECD as a whole. But this still leaves open the question whether tax changes of a similar order concentrated in *particular types* of (direct) taxation would or would not have similar effects. At any rate, so long as it is true that particular types of tax increase have bigger relative effects on the macroeconomic target in question than do others, it must be possible to find some ways of increasing taxation by a given amount that will have different relative effects on real output from others.

Table 3.3: Simulated effects on real GDP of changes in government non-wage expenditures and personal income tax cuts for the seven major OECD countries
(Five-year average of effect on rate of growth of real GDP as %ge of baseline, for a change over that period in the government's financial balance equal to 1% of GDP, with change in relation to rise in budget deficit in first year in parentheses)

	Rise in government non-wage expenditure	Cut in personal income tax
US	0.58 (4.12)	0.69 (4.11)
Japan	0.58 (3.50)	0.58 (3.30)
Germany	0.69 (3.89)	0.70 (3.89)
France	0.48 (3.46)	0.53 (3.55)
UK	0.38 (2.70)	0.39 (2.50)
Italy	0.39 (2.93)	0.47 (3.45)
Canada	0.31 (3.00)	0.29 (2.10)

The simulations used assume a fixed money supply and floating exchange rates.

Source: Figures for effects of government expenditures derived from Richardson (1987); figures for effects of personal income tax cuts supplied by that author on the basis of simulations analogous to those for government expenditures.

Taking these two considerations together, therefore, it may be possible to find combinations of (direct) tax increases that would have less effect on real GDP than government spending in general. The conclusions suggested by the results summarised in Tables 3.1 and 3.2 may be consistent with those that may be drawn from simulations with the OECD's Interlink model published in 1987. For, as Table 3.3 shows, over a five-year period changes in personal income tax had a somewhat greater effect on real GDP for a given effect on the government's financial balance over that period than did changes in government non-wage expenditures for five of the seven countries, though not for Canada, and Japan (for which the two effects were the same); but the difference was in most cases slight.

If however, the effects are related to the rise in the budget deficit *in the year that the measures are introduced*, government expenditure on non-wage items had the greater effect over the five years in four of the seven countries, while the two measures had the same effect in Germany. The effect of government non-wage expenditures is especially concentrated into the first two years (not shown in the table), over which period its effect on real GDP *exceeds* that of a cut in personal income tax having the same effect on the government's financial balance. It may be observed that over the full five year period, in which the effect of the income tax cuts is the greater in most of the countries, the differences between the results for the two measures in this simulation, where personal income tax alone is simulated on the tax side, are by no means as marked as they were in the simulation for the OECD as a whole, which used a *range* of direct taxation. This suggests that the other major form of direct taxation, social security contributions, presumably has a greater effect on real GDP than personal income tax for the same effect on the budget balance.

This contrast is more clearly marked between the results shown in Tables 3.1 and 3.2, on the one hand, and those that can be drawn from an earlier set of simulations with models from different countries, in response to a questionnaire from the OECD, which are summarised in Table 3.4.

It may be seen that for all these countries, except one of the two models for Canada, government non-wage expenditure clearly had a *greater* effect on real GDP/GNP than personal income tax cuts. (The effects on the budget balance for each year were not published; but the fiscal stimuli simulated are both equal to 1% of GDP/GNP. The closest comparison with the results shown in Table 3.3 would therefore be with the figures shown in parentheses in that table.)

One would expect, however, that if government outlays have the greater effect on real GDP, and would thus have a greater upward effect on tax receipts in subsequent years, this effect on revenue would to that extent reduce the budget deficit in those later years by more than would the extra revenue from the increase in growth resulting from income tax cuts. So far as this were true, the relative effect on GDP/GNP of government expenditure *per unit rise in the budget deficit over the whole five years* would thus be correspondingly *greater* relative to that of income tax cuts than Table 3.4 implies.

Table 3.4: Simulated effects on real GDP/GNP of certain OECD countries of government non-wage expenditures and personal income tax cuts
(%ge points change, average of Years 1, 2, 3 & 7 after the change of policy for a change in the budget deficit equal to 1% of GNP/GDP in Year 1)

	Government non-wage expenditure	Personal income tax cuts
US	0.89	0.82
Japan	2.35	1.41
France	1.62	0.65
UK	0.80	0.56
Canada 1	0.55	0.58
Canada 2	1.74	1.00
Australia	1.30	0.52
Netherlands	0.59	0.28
New Zealand*	0.25	0.11

*Average of Years 1, 3 & 5 only.

The simulations used are those with floating exchange rates and non-accommodating monetary policy – that is, one that allows interest rates to rise in response to expansionary fiscal measures.

Note: In the original, the simulations are for *increases* in personal income tax and *reductions* in government expenditure. The signs have therefore been reversed in the above table. The models used are those from individual countries, two different models being used for Canada.

Source: Derived from Chan-Lee and Kato (1984).

The differences between the results in Table 3.4 and those for the OECD as a whole in Tables 3.1 and 3.2 or the simulation for the major seven OECD countries individually in Table 3.3, may be largely the result of the differences in the models used for the simulations, and differences in point of detail in the definitions of government spending and taxation measures as between one country and another, as well as differences in the dates of the simulations, and therefore the data. Moreover, the simulations used in Table 3.1 assumed that real interest rates were kept constant (an 'accommodating' monetary policy), whereas that used in Table 3.3 and also Table 3.4 assumed a fixed money supply (that is, monetary policy was not accommodating). It should also be borne in mind that the results of the simulations used in Table 3.4 are expressed in *levels* of real GDP, whereas most of those in earlier tables are for *rates of change* in real GDP.

But the differences from Table 3.1 and 3.2 may also be due to the fact that results for individual countries may not necessarily be similar to those for a larger grouping such as the OECD as a whole; for more of the effect of a fiscal measure taken in one country may leak away than would be true for a larger grouping. Perhaps in an individual country more of the effects of cuts in income tax are likely to leak away through imports from other countries than are the effects of changes in government non-wage expenditures. The simulations reported in Table 3.3 (made with the OECD's Interlink model) would (like those reported in Tables 3.1 and 3.2) also take account of indirect repercussions upon the country adopting the policy measures through trade and other payments with other countries, whereas those in Table 3.4, using individual country models, are unlikely to have done so. So far as there is an apparent conflict between the results from the individual country model simulations drawn on in Table 3.4, and those with the OECD Interlink model drawn on in Table 3.3, it is probably defensible to take more account of the OECD's Interlink simulations, in view of their incorporation of indirect repercussions through their effects upon other countries.

But it should also be borne in mind that the definition of tax changes used in Tables 3.1 and 3.2 is broader than that used for the results in Tables 3.3 or 3.4 (which relate only to personal income tax changes, whereas the two earlier tables relate to a package of direct tax changes). This may well account for the fact that, in the simulations for the individual countries in Table 3.3, personal income tax cuts have a greater effect than changes in government non-wage expenditures in one country; in another the two effects are identical; and in other countries the difference is by no means as great as it is between government outlays and direct tax cuts in the simulations for the OECD as a whole.

A conclusion from the simulations discussed so far must therefore be that it is likely that, over a five-year period, though probably not over two or three years, a package of direct taxation measures (used for the simulations shown in Tables 3.1 and 3.2), has a greater effect on real GDP/GNP than do government non-wage expenditures for a given effect on the budget deficit; but that it is less likely that personal income tax changes do so; and that further evidence is required before one can make comparisons for individual countries between the effects of changes in broader definitions of government expenditure or changes in taxation generally.

EVIDENCE FOR THE EEC IN THE MID-1980s

Simulations by the secretariat of the then EEC in the mid-1980s, results derived from which are shown in Table 3.5, suggest that rises in public consumption had a greater effect on real GDP over the average of either three or five years (for a given rise in the budget deficit) than did cuts in household direct taxation, but less effect over five years (though not over three) than did cuts in either employers' social security contributions (national insurance contributions in Britain) or cuts in indirect taxation.

The effect of government consumption on the annual rate of growth over the whole five years was less than that of any of the other three measures, though it was greater over three years than a cut in employers' social security contributions or in direct taxation.

Over the whole five years, cuts in employers' social security contributions did most to increase the level of real GDP (though less than indirect tax cuts to increase the rate of growth), with indirect tax cuts increasing the level of real GDP more than either direct tax cuts or government consumption.

These results therefore imply that in choosing a fiscal instrument of expansion (or one to reduce its budget deficit) a government ought to consider whether it is interested mainly in the effects of the various instruments over three years or over five years; and whether it is interested mainly in their relative effects on the level of real GDP or its rate of growth.

Table 3.5: Simulated effects on level and rate of growth of real GDP of the EEC over five years of changes in various fiscal measures
(Average %ge change over five years for an annual average rise in budget deficit equal to 1% of GDP; effect over three years in parentheses)

	Level	Annual rate of growth
Cut in employers' social security contributions	1.80 (0.81)	0.20 (0.14)
Cut in indirect taxation	1.59 (1.17)	0.34 (0.56)
Rise in public consumption	1.26 (1.50)	0.14 (0.43)
Cut in household direct taxation	0.81 (0.62)	0.19 (0.29)

Source: Derived from Dramais (1986).

It may be seen from Table 3.6, however, that over the first year, or the first two years, government investment or consumption (the two not being differentiated in this simulation) has a markedly greater effect on real GDP than any of the forms of tax cut. Over the whole five years, however, the effects of changes in the first two forms of taxation exceed those of a rise in government consumption, the effects of which start to decline much more sharply than those of tax changes from year three onwards.

Table 3.6: Simulated effects on real GDP of the EEC of changes in various fiscal measures for a rise in the budget deficit in first year equal to 1% of GDP
(%ge points change)

	Year 1	Years 1 & 2	Years 1–5
Cuts in indirect taxation	0.44	0.82	5.66
Cuts in employers' social security contributions	0.33	0.60	5.00
Government investment or consumption	1.22	1.50	4.89
Cuts in household direct taxation	0.33	0.47	3.33

Source: As for Table 3.5.

The change in the budget balance (or PSBR) over the first year is often the main focus of discussion of a budget. Table 3.6 therefore relates the difference made to real GDP by the various measures to the *change in the budget balance during the first year of the change.*

For the EEC in the above simulations, it is cuts in indirect taxation, followed by cuts in employers' social security contributions, that have the greatest effect over the five years (for a given rise in the public sector deficit in the first year). But increases in government consumption still have a greater upward effect on the level of real GDP (though not on its average rate of growth) over the five years than do income tax cuts on this basis of comparison.

These results may well be consistent with the prima facie different results from the OECD shown in Tables 3.1, 3.2 and 3.3. This is partly because those results used a different definition on the side of government outlays – namely, non-wage expenditures, rather than public investment or consumption (which is used in the EEC simulation). Moreover, the OECD simulation used on the revenue side a package of direct taxation measures, which included employers' social security contributions as well as personal income tax. Taking the OECD and EEC results together, therefore, a reasonable conclusion from this evidence would be that it is changes in employers' social security or national insurance contributions that has most effect on real output (for a given effect on the budget deficit) over five years, rather than changes in personal income tax; and that government expenditures that include wages are likely to have a greater relative effect on real GDP than government non-wage expenditures alone.

SOME EVIDENCE FOR THE UNITED STATES

The simulations used as a basis for Table 3.7 were part of a paper appraising the US government's fiscal proposals in 1993. (It uses a computable general equilibrium model, MSG2, in contrast to the macroeconomic models that have been used in other tables.) These results (which relate to effects on the *level* of real GDP – rather than the *growth rates* that have been used predominantly in most earlier tables) strongly suggest that tax concessions for private investment and for a permanent labour tax credit (which may be thought of as analogous to cuts in employers' social security or national insurance contributions in Europe) had the greatest effect in stimulating real output for a given effect on the budget deficit. A cut in indirect taxation, followed by government infrastructure investment and then by a cut in corporation tax, would have the next greatest effect on output for a given effect on the budget deficit, and a temporary labour tax credit somewhat less.

Government infrastructure investment has more effect than government non-investment spending (which is termed 'military spending' in the model, and is not differentiated in its effects from other types of government spending apart from infrastructure investment); but clearly, on this evidence, over the five years as a whole both forms of government spending have less effect than the various types of tax concessions or reductions simulated, apart from the cut in corporation tax, or a cut in income taxation (in the form simulated here – which is a cut that mainly affects higher income groups, and which should therefore not be taken as indicative of the effects of a cut in income taxation generally, especially those of one concentrated in lower income groups, which would presumably have much greater stimulatory effects).

A cut in personal income tax in the US of the type simulated in Tables 3.3 and 3.4 (presumably a much wider range of income being affected than those in the McKibbin and Bagnoli simulations) had a greater effect on real GDP than a rise in government non-wage expenditures for a given effect on the budget balance over the whole five-year period. On the evidence of Tables 3.3 and 3.5, together with that in Table 3.7, therefore, a *general* cut in personal income tax should probably be placed somewhat below corporation tax, and above some or all types of government expenditures, in terms of its effects on real GDP for a given effect on the budget balance.

By comparison, the evidence in Table 3.4 was that government non-wage expenditure in the US had a somewhat larger effect on real GDP (over the total of the years 1, 2, 3 and 7 after the change) than cuts in personal income taxation – but the difference was not great, whereas government expenditures had an effect of the order of two to three times as large as do the type of personal income tax cuts simulated by McKibbin and Bagnoli.

Table 3.7 also shows the simulated effects of these measures over three years. It may be seen that the ranking of the measures is not radically different over this shorter period, except that a corporation tax cut has a much smaller effect than government spending over this shorter period, and government investment spending has a relatively greater effect over the shorter period than the longer one.

Table 3.7: Simulated effects of various fiscal measures on US GDP
for a given effect on the budget deficit
(%ge deviation of real GDP from trend relative to deviation of
budget deficit from trend as percentage of GDP, five-year totals,
with three-year totals in parentheses)

	Change in level of real GDP
Permanent investment tax credit	3.32 (2.29)
Temporary investment tax credit	2.38 (2.58)
Permanent labour tax credit	1.88 (2.20)
Cut in value-added tax	1.69 (2.47)
Temporary labour tax credit	1.07 (2.45)
Government infrastructure investment (cut-off)	0.82 (1.02)
Government infrastructure investment (gradual)	0.75 (0.74)
Corporation tax cut	0.55 (0.73)
Non-investment government spending*	0.56 (0.29)
Lump-sum transfers to households	0.39 (0.23)
Income tax cut	0.23 (0.35)

* The figures for non-investment spending are derived from those for cuts in military expenditure in the original (with the signs reversed). The model does not distinguish between military expenditure and other types of non-investment government expenditure. The assumptions about the changes in this item made in the original are that there is a lag between the time that the changes are announced and the time they are implemented. The figures given here are therefore for the five years or three years beginning *two years after* the changes are announced, so as to make this item more nearly comparable with the other items in the table.

Source: Derived from graphs in McKibbin and Bagnoli (1993) and data supplied by them.

The effects on the average annual rate of growth of real GDP over five years for 1% of GDP rise in the budget deficit (not shown in the table) are greatest for a cut in indirect taxation, followed by non-investment government spending and a permanent labour tax credit. The income tax cuts simulated had a small upward effect on the average annual rate of growth, as did a cut in corporation tax and transfers to households. But the other measures all reduced the annual average rate of growth over the period, even though all these measures raised the annual average *level* of real GDP over the period.

The simulations by Knoester cited below (Tables 3.10 and 3.11) provide conflicting evidence as to whether government expenditure has a greater or smaller effect on real GDP than do cuts in direct taxation; but in neither case is the difference between the two anywhere near as great as that which is shown for the US by the figures in Table 3.7 between government spending and the type of personal income tax cuts simulated there. The fairest conclusion on this point seems therefore to be that a general cut in direct taxation in the US may have somewhat more or somewhat less effect on real GDP than a rise in government spending having the same effect on the budget balance; but that general personal income tax cuts probably have less effect than the other types of tax cut simulated by McKibbin and Bagnoli; and that over three years the other principal form of direct taxation, corporation tax, has a greater effect on real GDP than do some forms of government spending.

EVIDENCE FROM UK MODELS

The most recent University of Warwick simulations with UK models available at the time of writing suggest that, for a given change in the PSBR in the first year after the change, all three of those models for which the simulation shows that both these fiscal measures increase the PSBR suggest that an income tax cut raises output by less than does a rise in government expenditure for a given rise in the PSBR in the first year. The NIESR simulation shows government expenditure as raising output by more than do income tax cuts for a given *fall* in the PSBR, and Compact suggests that government spending reduces the PSBR in the process of increasing output by more than do income tax cuts (which increase the PSBR in the process of raising output).

The balance of this evidence is thus that government outlays raise output more than do income tax cuts for a given effect on the PSBR. Some of the evidence even suggests that the association in the public mind of expansionary fiscal measures with an increased PSBR (especially in the year the decisions are taken) may be the opposite of the truth − at least in respect of certain fiscal measures; and that combinations of government outlays and income tax cuts could certainly be found that would increase real output while reducing the PSBR (and also combinations of them that would increase the

PSBR while reducing output). All the simulations imply that, for a given change in the PSBR, it makes a substantial difference to the effect on real output whether one provides any stimulus by an increase in government outlays or by cuts in income tax.

Table 3.8: Simulated effects on real GDP of the UK of government expenditure and income tax cuts

(Total of Years 1, 3 and 5 for a billion pounds change in PSBR in Year 1)

Model	LBS	NIESR*	HMT	OEF	COMPACT*
Income tax cut	0.30	0.21*	0.12	0.19	7.50*
Government spending**	0.77	3.19*	0.42	0.62	27.20*

Key to names of models: LBS=London Business School; NIESR=National Institute of Economic and Social Research; HMT=Her Majesty's Treasury; OEF=Oxford Economic Forecasting; COMPACT is the model provided by Strathclyde University.

* In the NIESR model, both a rise in government expenditure and an income tax cut *reduce* the PSBR (expressed in that model as a percentage point deviation from trend in the ratio of the PSBR to GDP) in the first year. The figures shown for that model are for the rise in real GDP for a given *fall* in the PSBR in Year 1. For the simulation with the Compact model, the rise in government spending reduces the PSBR (expressed in the model in terms of the rise in the debt/GDP ratio in Year 1), whereas the income tax cut increases it. The figures for government outlays in that simulation thus show the rise in real GDP associated with a given *fall* in the PSBR, and those for an income tax cut show the increase in GDP for a given *rise* in the PSBR.
** Simulation with fiscal solvency rule suppressed.

Source: Derived from Church et al. (1995).

The results of simulations made by the Macroeconomic Modelling Bureau of the University of Warwick two years earlier with various models of the UK economy (a slightly different set of models from those used in 1995) are somewhat less difficult to interpret, for in each model real GDP rises over the five-year period with both income tax cuts and increases in government spending, as does also the PSBR (in the first year and also over the five years as a whole).

In this set of simulations, which is drawn upon in Table 3.9 (a set of simulations that is less recent, but which covers more models and more policy changes than those reported in Table 3.8) the balance of the evidence is that a rise in government expenditure raises real GDP by more for a given rise in the PSBR than do income tax cuts over the five-year period (whether in relation to the rise in the PSBR over the full five years or to that in the first

year alone – though figures relating the effects to changes in the PSBR in
the first year are not shown in this table). In four of the models that is clearly
true, though in the other two models income tax cuts are more expansionary
in this sense. If one considers only the median or average results for all the
models for each policy instrument, the rise in government outlays is in this
sense clearly the most expansionary of the four instruments simulated.

This evidence also suggests that cuts in VAT are on this measure more
expansionary than cuts in income tax or in employers' national insurance
contributions. As those three forms of tax account for the overwhelming
majority of taxation in Britain, it seems reasonable to conclude from this
evidence that in Britain government expenditure is likely to raise real GDP
over a five-year period by more than most forms of packages of tax cuts. In
a majority of models, and using the average or median, changes in national
insurance contributions have a greater effect than do changes in income tax
(at any rate in the form simulated – which is a penny off the standard rate).

Table 3.9: Simulated effects on rate of increase in real GDP of the UK of
various fiscal measures
(Five-year totals per billion pounds rise in PSBR at 1990 prices)

	Rate of growth of real GDP							
Model:	LBS	NIESR	HMT	BE	OEF	STR	Average	Median
Rise in government spending	0.70	0.60	0.32	1.47	0.78	0.30	0.45	0.64
Cut in VAT	0.07	0.42	0.24	0.79	0.93	0.48	0.49	0.45
Cut in employers' national insurance contributions	0.17	0.26	0.28	0.93	0.38	0.41	0.40	0.33
Cut in income tax	0.12	0.52	0.14	0.28	0.33	0.92	0.38	0.30

Key to models: LBS=London Business School; NIESR=National Institute of Economic
and Social Research; HMT=Her Majesty's Treasury; BE=Bank of England; STR=
Model provided by Strathclyde University.
Nominal interest rates are assumed to be held constant by monetary policy.

Source: Derived from Church et al. (1993).

EVIDENCE FOR THE US, JAPAN AND EUROPE

It may be seen from Table 3.10 that, for each country or group, in the first year the effect of a rise in public spending upon real GDP exceeds that of a cut in direct taxation (for a given change in the budget deficit). In year 5 this is again (marginally) true for the US and for Japan, but for Europe the effect of the rise in direct taxation upon real GDP has now come to exceed that of a rise in public spending. Again, it should be borne in mind that this simulation is for a wider range of direct taxation (including social security contributions by employers) than that used in the simulations of income tax changes in the UK models reported in Tables 3.6 and 3.7, or for the results with various national models reported in Table 3.4, or for the EEC in Table 3.5. These various results may be consistent with one another if it is forms of direct taxation other than personal income tax changes that have the greatest effect on real GDP (as the EEC simulations suggest). It could also be relevant that the OECD uses a narrower definition of government expenditure – on non-wage items only – than the definition used in the simulation the results of which are shown in Table 3.9.

Table 3.10: *Simulated effects on real GDP of the US, Japan and Europe*
of direct tax cuts and increases in public spending
(%ge points change in Years 1 and 5 for a rise in the budget deficit equal
to 1% of GDP in the same year)

	US		Japan		Europe	
	Year 1	Year 5	Year 1	Year 5	Year 1	Year 5
Cut in direct taxation	0.50	1.17	0.53	1.03	0.33	1.12
Public spending increases	1.85	1.20	1.47	2.25	1.23	0.72

Note: Signs are reversed from the original, which was for cuts in government spending and increases in direct taxation.

Source: Derived from Knoester (1988).

There is another reason why it is somewhat difficult to compare these results with those for the whole OECD. This is that results for years 1 and 5 only are given in the simulation reported in Table 3.10, whereas results for each year are given in the simulations by the OECD using its own model. But so far as this evidence goes, and in contrast to the OECD results, it supports the traditional view that government spending has a greater effect on GDP than (direct) taxation for the same effect on the budget balance. The balance of the evidence for the UK shown in Table 3.9 implied that changes in VAT also had a greater effect on real GDP than changes in employers' social security contributions or personal income tax.

EVIDENCE FOR THREE MAJOR COUNTRIES AND ONE SMALLER COUNTRY

It may be seen from Table 3.11 that this simulation showed that the effect of an equal rise in both government spending and direct taxes (including social security contributions) was negative in each case. In other words, the effect of a rise in direct taxation (including social security contributions) on output exceeds that of an equal rise in government spending. This is a similar result to that shown in Tables 3.1 and 3.2 for the whole of the OECD, which was also for a package of direct tax increases, but only for non-wage government expenditures. This suggests that the balanced budget multiplier (for government spending in general coupled with a rise in a package of direct taxation) may be negative (at least for these countries). The evidence for the EEC shown in Tables 3.5 and 3.6 could be consistent with this, as these tables showed that the effect on real output of rises in employers' social security contributions was greatly in excess of that of income tax changes, and also in excess of that of changes in government consumption, for the same rise in the budget deficit over a five-year period.

It would, however, be difficult to reconcile the outcome shown in Table 3.11 with the results for the UK shown in Tables 3.8 and 3.9, where the effect of government spending was, in almost all models, in excess of that of employers' national insurance contributions or personal income tax changes having the same effect on the PSBR. But as the simulations for the UK did not include company tax, that may account for the difference from the outcome of the simulation of a package of direct taxation shown in Table 3.11.

Table 3.11: Simulated effects on volume of production in Germany, the Netherlands, the UK and the US of a rise in public spending and in direct taxes plus social security contributions each equal to 1% of GDP (%ge change)

	Germany		Netherlands		UK		US	
Year:	1	5	1	5	1	5	1	5
	−0.4	−2.6	−0.4	−1.4	−0.2	−1.2	−0.3	−1.0

Source: Knoester (1995).

Moreover, the evidence for the US in Table 3.10 appears to be in conflict with that shown in Table 3.11, which draws on other simulations of Knoester, and which shows that government spending had a *smaller* effect on real GDP than direct tax cuts having the same effect on the budget balance (at least in years 1 and 5 – the only years covered).

EVIDENCE FOR SOME SMALLER COUNTRIES

Evidence for Some Nordic Countries

It may be seen from Table 3.12 that in three of the five models (two of the models being for Finland), and also taking an average for the four countries, government expenditure on employment has a greater effect on real GDP than does a cut in local income tax. (The evidence on this point for Finland from the two models for that country is conflicting.) Taking the average of the four countries, government employment expenditure appears to have the greatest effect on real GDP of the three measures tested, followed by cuts in local income tax and then cuts in VAT.

Table 3.12: Simulated effects on real GDP of various fiscal measures in four Nordic countries
(Totals for Years 1, 2, 3 & 5 of %ge deviation of real GDP from baseline for a given deviation from baseline in general government financial balance, as a % of GDP)

Model:	ADAM	MODAG	KOSMOS	KESSU	BOF4	Average*
Government employment expenditure	1.76	5.09	5.13	1.73	1.29	3.37
Cut in VAT	3.77	0.36	0.85	1.21	0.66	1.48
Cut in local income tax	4.19	0.54	1.09	1.60	2.58	1.98

Key to models: ADAM=Department of the Budget, Denmark; MODAG=Central Bureau of Statistics, Norway; KOSMOS=National Institute of Economic Research, Sweden; KESSU=Ministry of Finance, Finland; BOF4=Bank of Finland.
   *Taking the average of the two models for Finland as one case.
   Note: It has been confirmed by the authors that the results they give of the simulations for local income tax are in fact for a *reduction* (whereas the table in the original states that it is for an *increase*). The signs in this table are those appropriate to a reduction.

Source: Derived from Wallis and Whitley (1991).

Evidence for Belgium and the Netherlands

It may be seen from Table 3.13 that changes in employment in the public sector and in state investment in Belgium were found in this simulation to have the greatest effect on real GDP, followed by social security transfers, while changes in personal income tax and in VAT had appreciably less effect than any of those, but appreciably more than cuts in employers' social security contributions.

Again, as with some of the results for Nordic countries, these results may perhaps be reconciled with those reported above relating to the OECD as a whole (Tables 3.1 and 3.2), which related to *non-wage* government expenditures, if these have appreciably less effect on real GDP than government expenditure on employment or public investment; especially as the effect of social security transfers to households (presumably the main non-wage government expenditure, and therefore closest of the items in this table to the outlay item used in the OECD simulation – non-wage government expenditures) is less than either of the other government outlays simulated here. Both personal income tax cuts and the other direct tax change simulated here – employers' social security contributions – have a very small effect compared with the two types of government outlay simulated here. But personal income tax changes have a greater effect on real GDP than do changes in VAT or employers' social security contributions.

Table 3.13: Simulated effects on real GDP of various fiscal measures in Belgium
(Five-year totals of %ge change of GDP from baseline for 1% of
GDP deviation from baseline of budget deficit)

	Change in real GDP
Rise in total employment in the public sector	0.98
Rise in state investment	0.76
Rise in social security transfers to households	0.54
Cut in personal income tax	0.39
Cut in VAT on consumption	0.32
Cut in employers' social security contributions	0.13

Source: Derived from Bogaert et al. (1990).

The results for Belgium are consistent in some respects (but not in others) with the results for the EEC as a whole reported in Tables 3.5 and 3.6. For each item that is simulated in both sets of results, the relative effect on output for a given change in the budget balance is, as one might expect for a small open economy, a good deal less for Belgium than for the EEC as a whole. But the measures of government outlay simulated for Belgium have a greater relative effect on real GDP than either cuts in personal income tax rates or cuts in indirect taxation or in employers' social security contributions – the last of which ranks at the top in the results for the EEC as a whole, though at the bottom in the results of the simulation for Belgium. So far as these results reflect real differences between Belgium, on the one hand, and the whole EEC on the other, a likely explanation is that in a small open economy such as that of Belgium a large proportion of the spending resulting from cuts in employers' social security contributions, or in income tax and VAT, may leak away to other countries; whereas for the EEC as a whole a much higher proportion of the expenditure in question would remain within this much larger area.

By contrast, a much higher proportion of public sector expenditure (to some extent on investment, but especially on public sector employment) than that resulting from tax cuts could be expected to result in a stimulus to output within Belgium.

Table 3.14: Simulated effects on volume of production of the Netherlands of various fiscal measures
(%ge effect for change equal to 1% of GDP in each fiscal measure)

	Change in volume of production	
	Year 1	Year 5
Equal cut of 1% of GDP in public spending and direct taxation	−0.2*	0.4*
Equal cut in indirect taxation and public spending	0.1*	0.8*
Effect of an indirect tax cut *less* effect of a direct tax cut	0.3*	0.4*
Equal cut in public investment and direct taxation	−0.3	0.0

* Average of all available models for the Netherlands.

Source: Derived from Knoester and Kolodziejak (1994) and Knoester (1995).

In the Netherlands (Table 3.14), in the first year, the downward effect on the volume of output (presumably meaning real GDP – though this is not stated in the original source) of the cut in public spending generally is greater than the stimulus due to the cut in direct taxation. The bottom line shows, however, that if it were public sector investment that was cut, the downward effect on output would by the fifth year after the change of policy be as great as the stimulatory effect of the cut in direct taxation. It is therefore clear that public sector investment has, on these figures, by the fifth year, an appreciably greater effect on output than does government consumption spending, and much the same effect as a change in direct taxation (here including employers' social security contributions). The argument (made by Knoester in various publications) that a balanced budget reduction is expansionary in terms of its effect on production thus depends (according to these figures) partly on what types of public expenditure are cut. For one could come to his conclusion (on the basis of his figures) only if the public expenditure cut was made up of consumption (or of some combinations of public expenditure that included both investment and consumption), but not if it were solely public investment.

Moreover, his figures in this and an earlier simulation also suggest that the stimulatory effects on output of a cut in indirect taxation are greater than the downward impact on output of an equal cut in government spending, though only to a small extent in the first year. The stimulatory effect of a balanced budget reduction that involves cuts in indirect taxation on the revenue side is, on these figures, clearly greater than one involving cuts in direct taxation. In other words, the effect on real output of changes in the level of the various forms of direct taxation used in this simulation is less than that of an equal cut in indirect taxation. From the EEC simulation reported in Tables 3.5 and 3.6, it may be seen that for this larger area employers' social security contributions and personal income tax changes had a greater effect on real GDP than changes in indirect taxation – a larger proportion of which presumably leaked away towards other countries through imports for the small open economy of the Netherlands.

Evidence for Portugal

It may be seen from Table 3.15 that, of the four measures simulated, the greatest effect on upon real GDP for the first year is that of expenditure on public sector employment, followed by that of a rise in public investment. Cuts in both direct and indirect taxation have a much smaller effect (though their relative effect rises slightly over the first five years as a whole). In the long run, public investment expenditure has by far the greatest effect on real GDP, followed by public sector employment. For this country, at any rate, the available evidence is that public expenditure has a greater effect on real GDP than either of the two types of taxation simulated, over both longer and shorter periods. Direct tax changes have, over the longer period, rather more effect than indirect tax changes for a given effect on the budget balance.

Again, a comparison may be made with the simulation in Table 3.1 for the whole of the OECD of changes in government non-wage expenditure and in direct taxation. It is clear that government expenditures that included employment (which would constitute part of the figures in Table 3.15 for public investment) might have a bigger effect on real GDP in Portugal than non-wage expenditures. The smaller magnitude of the effect of income tax cuts can be reconciled with the relatively large effect of direct tax changes for the whole OECD partly by the fact that a wider range of direct taxation is included in the simulation for the whole of the OECD, and partly by the fact that, as Portugal is a small economy, a relatively large part of the stimulatory effect of tax cuts (compared with those covering the whole of the OECD, and also by comparison with government spending on investment and employment) might be expected to leak away towards imports. (We saw earlier that this appeared also to be true for Belgium and the Netherlands.)

Table 3.15: Simulated effects of various fiscal measures on level of real GDP of Portugal
(%ge deviation from baseline of real GDP for a change in public borrowing equal to 1% of GDP)

	Year 1	Years 1–5	Year 15
Rise in public sector employment	2.15	1.57	1.49
Rise in public investment	2.01	1.44	2.71
Cut in direct taxation of households	0.44	0.58	0.59
Cut in indirect taxation	0.49	0.46	0.44

Note that the actual figures are provided only for the first of the five years and for Year 15 (and also a still later year) in the original source; but there is a graphical representation of the results for the other years, which has been used here to provide approximate figures for the first five years.

Source: Derived from Modesto and Neves (1995).

Evidence for Ireland and Spain

As with the case of Portugal considered in earlier paragraphs, from the results for both Spain (Herce and Sosvilla-Rivero, 1995) and Ireland (Bradley et al., 1995) in the Hermin model for countries on the EU periphery there is some evidence to suggest that the effect on GDP of both government infrastructure investment and of public employment is substantially in excess of that of indirect taxation changes, as Table 3.16 shows.

Table 3.16 shows that public employment expenditure has a greater effect on real GDP than public investment in both countries, and that both have a much greater effect than an indirect tax cut. This ranking of instruments appears to be more or less in conformity with other simulations above (in those cases where the categories of taxation and expenditure are comparable), except those that find that indirect tax changes have a greater effect on real GDP than some forms of public expenditure. It does, moreover, appear to be consistent with the results for other small open economies, in that much of the effect of tax changes probably leaks away into imports, whereas less of the effect of public expenditure changes appears to do so.

Table 3.16: Simulated effects on real GDP of various fiscal measures in Ireland and Spain
(Five-year average of %ge points change for change in public borrowing equal to 1% of GDP)

	Level of real GDP	
	Ireland	Spain
Public employment	1.40	1.05
Public investment	1.07	0.93
Indirect tax cut	0.38	0.58

Source: Derived from graphical data in Bradley et al. (1995) and Herce and Sosvilla-Rivero (1995).

CONCLUSION: THE RANKING OF FISCAL MEASURES IN TERMS OF THEIR EFFECTS ON REAL GDP

The balance of the evidence from the various simulations drawn upon in this chapter suggests the following tentative ranking in terms of the effect of the various fiscal measures simulated for a given effect on the budget balance, over a period of five years. The measures are ranked with those having the greatest effect on real GDP for a given effect on the budget balance at the top of the list.

Not all the evidence in the various simulations discussed in this chapter would be consistent with this ranking, which is based on a judgement as to the probable relative ranking on the balance of this evidence. (Readers may like to make their own judgement about the ranking by reference to the results of the various simulations discussed in this chapter. To facilitate this process, brief summaries of the ranking for each table are shown in Table 3.18.) It is also to be remembered that the evidence for smaller countries showed that for them tax cuts, perhaps especially indirect tax cuts, appeared to have less of their effect within the country than did most forms of government spending.

Table 3.17: Ranking of various fiscal measures in different tables in terms of their effects on real GDP for a 1% of GDP change in the budget deficit
(Most expansionary over five years for a given change in the budget balance at the top)

1	Rises in government expenditure on employment
2	Rises in government investment expenditure
3	Tax concessions for private investment
4	Labour tax credit
5	Cuts in value-added tax
6	Cuts in social security or national insurance contributions by employers
7	Cuts in company or corporation tax
8	Rises in government non-wage expenditure
9	Rises in government consumption
10	Rises in social security transfers
11	Cuts in personal income tax

Note that some of these categories are overlapping, especially the various subcategories of government expenditure.

Some policy implications of the ranking order will be discussed in Chapter 9. For the present it may suffice to point out that a government wishing to give the maximum stimulus for the minimum upward effect on its borrowing will opt for some combination of cuts in those taxes (or rises in government outlays) near to the top of the table, combined with increases in those taxes (or cuts in those government outlays) nearer to the bottom of the table. It should, however, be stressed that the ranking may well vary considerably from country to country or from one group of countries to another, as well as with the period over which the effect is measured. In particular, public infrastructure investment and some other forms of government spending appear at or near the bottom of the list for the US, but at the top of the list for most of the others.

Table 3.18: Ranking of measures in different tables

Tables 3.1 & 3.2 (OECD)	Table 3.3 (7 major OECD countries)	Table 3.4 (various OECD countries)	Tables 3.5 & 3.6 (EEC)	Table 3.7 (US)	Tables 3.8 & 3.9 (UK)
Package of cuts in income tax & social security contributions	Income tax cuts	Government non-wage expenditure	Cut in social security contributions	Investment tax credit	Cut in VAT
	Government non-wage expenditure	Income tax cuts	Cut in VAT	Labour tax credit	Government spending
Government non-wage expenditure			Government expenditure	Cut in indirect tax	Cut in national insurance contributions
			Income tax cuts	Government investment	Income tax cuts
				Corporation tax cut	
				Government consumption	
				Transfers to households	
				Income tax cuts	

Table 3.10 (US, Japan (& Europe)	Table 3.11 (US, UK, Germany, Netherlands)	Table 3.12 (Nordic countries)	Table 3.13 (Belgium)	Table 3.14 (Netherlands)	Table 3.15 (Portugal)	Table 3.16 (Ireland & Spain)
Direct tax cuts	Direct tax cuts	Government employment expenditure	Public employment	Public investment	Public employment	Public employment
Government spending	Government spending	Cut in VAT	Public investment	Indirect tax cuts	Public investment	Public investment
		Cut in local income tax	Social security transfers	Income tax cuts	Income tax cuts	Cut in VAT
			Income tax cuts	Public consumption	Cut in VAT	
			Cut in VAT			
			Cut in social security contributions			

4 Effects on Employment and Unemployment

It is insufficient for governments to consider only the effects of alternative fiscal measures upon total output (as indicated by real GDP or GNP). Quite apart from the difficulties of measuring real GDP or GNP accurately (perhaps especially that part of it produced by governments), there are more fundamental reasons why a government should be concerned with the effects on employment and unemployment of alternative combinations of fiscal measures, and not only with their effect on real GNP.

In particular, as effects on GNP may be sub-divided into (i) effects on output per head (usually per person employed) and (ii) effects on the number of people employed, attention to only the first of these risks ignoring the welfare consequences of any rise in output per person employed that is achieved at the expense of the numbers of people in employment. As different combinations of fiscal measures having the same effect on the budget deficit or surplus may have different effects on productivity (as measured by output per person employed), comparisons of their effects should also take account of their relative effects on employment and unemployment. It is those effects that will be considered in this chapter.

Not all the simulations drawn upon in Chapter 3 provide indications of the relative effects of various fiscal measures on employment or unemployment; but where these results are available, they are drawn upon in this chapter.

EVIDENCE FOR THE OECD AS A WHOLE

It may be concluded from Table 4.1 relating to the OECD as a whole, that by the fifth year after the change of policy, government non-wage outlays have a much smaller downward effect on unemployment than do cuts in a package of direct taxation (including not only personal income tax but also employers' social security contributions).

A similar picture emerges from the simulation (for a different pattern over time of changes in government non-wage expenditures and direct taxation) summarised in Table 4.2. Over a five-year period, changes in the package of direct taxation have a greater effect on unemployment than do changes in government non-wage expenditures for a given effect on the government net lending or borrowing (the budget deficit), both over the five years and the three years as a whole, as well as in the fifth year after the change (though the effects are the same for the two measures in the third year).

Table 4.1: Simulated effects on unemployment rate of the OECD of a rise in government non-wage expenditures and cuts in direct taxation, with an accommodating monetary policy
(Five-year totals of %ge points effect on unemployment rate for
a fall in government net lending equal to 1% of GDP in the same period,
with change in fifth year in parentheses)

Government non-wage expenditures	Cuts in direct taxes
−0.56 (−0.57)	−0.87 (−0.82)

The simulation used is that with unchanged real interest rates (that is, an accommodating monetary policy).

The years covered are five years beginning in the third year after the first change in policy, no changes in the budget deficit or items affecting it having been assumed in the first two years.

Source: Derived from Richardson et al. (1994).

Table 4.2: Simulated effects on unemployment rate of the OECD of government non-wage expenditures and cuts in direct taxation, with a non-accommodating monetary policy
(Three-year and five-year totals of %ge points change for a 1% of GDP/GNP
rise in budget deficit, with change in Years 3 & 5 in parentheses)

Government non-wage expenditures		Cuts in direct taxation	
5 years	3 years	5 years	3 years
−0.02 (−0.14)	−0.27 (−0.29)	−0.09 (0.33)	−0.45 (−0.29)

Source: Derived from Leibfritz et al. (1994).

Table 4.3 shows a similar (but earlier) simulation for each of the seven major OECD countries, also using the OECD Interlink model, but using cuts in personal income tax only, rather than a package of direct tax cuts. It may be seen that, over five years, in five of the countries the effect of the non-wage government outlays on employment was *greater* than that of cuts in personal income tax, but that the reverse was true for the US, while for Canada the effect of government non-wage expenditure on employment was the same as that of personal income tax cuts having the same effect on the budget balance. For Japan neither measure had any effect on unemployment. For all the other countries except Italy government non-wage expenditure had a slightly greater effect than personal income tax cuts in reducing unemployment. But over the first three years after the change, in every country except Japan, government non-wage expenditures reduced unemployment by more than did cuts in personal income tax having the same effect on the budget balance.

Table 4.3: Simulated effects on unemployment rate and employment in major OECD countries of a rise in government non-wage expenditure and a cut in personal income tax
(Five-year totals of %ge points change in unemployment rate over five years or %ge change in employment for 1% of GDP fiscal shock, with change over three years in parentheses)

	Effect on unemployment rate (percentage points)		%ge effect on employment	
	Government non-wage expenditures	Cut in income tax	Government non-wage expenditures	Cut in income tax
US	−0.23 (−0.41)	−0.22 (−0.32)	0.23 (0.44)	0.31 (0.46)
Japan	0.00 (0.00)	0.00 (0.00)	0.13 (0.19)	0.12 (0.16)
Germany	−0.25 (−0.37)	−0.24 (−0.26)	0.33 (0.44)	0.31 (0.30)
France	−0.12 (−0.10)	−0.11 (−0.08)	0.18 (0.17)	0.15 (0.30)
UK	−0.28 (−0.36)	−0.22 (−0.25)	0.32 (0.45)	0.27 (0.31)
Italy	−0.00 (−0.10)	−0.09 (−0.07)	0.13 (0.10)	0.10 (0.12)
Canada	−0.21 (−0.35)	−0.15 (−0.20)	0.18 (0.46)	0.18 (0.29)

The simulation used assumes a fixed money supply and floating exchange rates.

Source: Derived from Richardson (1987) and data supplied by him.

One reason for differences between the results in Table 4.3 and those in Tables 4.1 and 4.2 is presumably that the taxation changes assumed in the simulations for the OECD as a whole were for a wider range of direct tax changes than that used in the simulations for the seven major OECD countries, which were for changes in personal income tax only. Presumably in Europe changes in employers' social security contributions had more effect on unemployment than did changes in income tax (which is confirmed by the EEC simulation referred to below).

It may also be that circumstances changed between the mid-1980s and the mid-1990s, in such a way that direct tax changes came to have a greater effect on employment and unemployment than did government non-wage expenditures. For example, the high level of employers' social security contributions in European countries might by the mid-1990s have come to increase business costs so much as to exert greater downward pressure on employment from the cost side (as well as by way of direct reductions in demand). This would accentuate the effects upon unemployment of the package of direct tax changes that includes those contributions, by comparison with that shown in the simulation using personal income tax changes alone.

Table 4.4 shows the results from simulations carried out with different models for each of a number of countries in response to a questionnaire from the OECD in the mid-1980s. It may be seen that, for all the countries for which results for both government non-wage expenditure and personal income tax cuts are available from this source, government non-wage expenditure had the greater effect in reducing unemployment. (This is also true of both the models for Canada, whereas we saw in Chapter 3 that in one of these models income tax cuts had a bigger effect on real GDP than a rise in government non-wage expenditure of the same size.)

Table 4.4 suggests that in all these countries rises in government non-wage real expenditure reduced unemployment over the period simulated by more than did personal income tax cuts for the same initial effect on the budget balance.

These simulation results are not, however, exactly comparable with most of those used in earlier tables, in the sense that those used in Table 4.4 do not give the change in government borrowing for each year, whereas the other simulations used above do so. The effect on the government's fiscal balance in the initial year is, however, the same for the cut in direct taxation as it is for government non-wage expenditures; and it would not be likely that the ranking of these two instruments would vary if their effects on unemployment were related instead to the change in government borrowing over the whole period.

It may well be, of course, that the use of different models for different countries for the results given in Table 4.4 (rather than the single model for the whole of the OECD used in the simulation summarised in Tables 4.1 and 4.2) is the main reason for the difference of the ranking of the two measures from the results shown in Tables 4.1 and 4.2. It is, however, interesting and probably significant that such a wide range of different models for different countries all give the result that government non-wage expenditures had a greater effect in reducing unemployment than did cuts in personal income tax. Another partial explanation for the difference between these two tables might be that more of the effect of the measures taken in individual countries would leak away to other countries through imports than would be true for a much larger (and to that extent less open) economy such as the OECD as a whole; but for this to reverse the ranking of these two measures it would be necessary for more of the stimulus resulting from tax cuts than that from government non-wage expenditures in an individual country to leak away to the rest of the world; and for the OECD as a whole for a much smaller proportion of taxation than of government outlays to leak away in the form of imports from outside the area.

Table 4.4: Simulated effects on unemployment rate in various OECD countries of government non-wage expenditure and income tax cuts
(%ge points change from baseline for a 1% of GDP fiscal shock, average of Years 1, 2, 3 & 7 after the change of policy)

	Government real non-wage expenditure	Personal income tax cuts
US	−0.34	−0.28
Japan	−0.06	−0.03
France	−0.35	−0.15
UK	−0.33	−0.27
Canada 1	−0.29	−0.27
Canada 2	−0.83	−0.50
Australia	−0.67	−0.43
Netherlands	−0.27	−0.15

The simulations used are those with floating exchange rates and a non-accommodating monetary policy (a fixed money supply).
Note: In the original, the simulations are for *increases* in personal income tax and *reductions* in government expenditure.

Source: Derived from Chan-Lee and Kato (1984).

Perhaps a more important explanation is that the OECD model uses a wider definition of direct taxation, including employers' social security contributions. It is also likely that employers' social security contributions have become quantitatively more important in the years between the mid-1980s (when the individual country simulations were undertaken) and 1994 (when the simulations for the OECD as a whole were made).

Table 4.5 shows the results of a simulation made in the later 1980s for the effects on unemployment in the US, Japan and 'Europe' (defined as the EEC as it was at the time) of *reductions* in both direct taxation and government spending generally.

The simulations are for a cut in both direct taxation and public spending each equal to 1% of the wages bill.

It may be seen from this table that the effect of public spending in reducing unemployment is in each case greater (for a given effect on the budget deficit) than that of direct tax cuts in the first year; and for the US that is also true for year 5. But for Europe, on this simulation, the effect on unemployment of government expenditure had become negligible by year 5, although tax changes were still affecting unemployment in the expected direction.

It does not, therefore, seem likely on these figures that for Japan and the US (and also Europe in the first year), if the aim is to reduce unemployment over the whole period, it will be possible to do so by decreasing government outlays and direct taxes equally (whereas that would, on the comparable simulation, be appropriate if the aim was to have the effect of increasing real GDP, as we saw in Table 3.10).

These conclusions are qualified by simulations by the same author for some individual countries (in Table 4.6).

Table 4.5: Simulated effects on unemployment rate in the US, Japan and Europe of public spending and cuts in direct taxes
(%ge points for a change in the budget deficit equal to
1% of GDP in the same year)

	US		Japan		Europe	
	Year 1	Year 5	Year 1	Year 5	Year 1	Year 5
Cut in direct taxation	–0.15	–0.87	–0.22	–0.30	–0.12	–0.33
Public spending increase	–0.74	–1.36	–0.06	–0.37	–0.33	0.00

Source: Derived from Knoester (1988).

Table 4.6 shows that a balanced budget increase (taking the form of a rise in government expenditure and a rise in direct taxation) has an *upward* effect on unemployment in each of these countries for the two years in question, except for the US in year 1; that is, that the rise in direct taxation has a greater effect in increasing unemployment than the rise in government spending has in reducing it.

But the same table shows that for the US a cut in direct taxation would reduce unemployment more than does a rise in government expenditure by the fifth year after the change, but not in the first year.

Clearly, one cannot assess the relative effects of the two measures over the whole five-year period at all exactly from these two years alone; but for the US in the first year this result – that government spending has a greater effect than direct tax cuts – may seem to be in conflict with that found in Table 4.3. Again, the fact that the simulation drawn upon in Table 4.6 (as in Table 4.5) uses a wider range of direct taxation than the personal income tax changes simulated in Table 4.3 could well be a large part of the explanation. As corporation tax and, in recent years, payroll taxes are the principal other direct taxes in the US, this may mean that changes in corporation tax and payroll taxes have a greater effect on unemployment than do changes in personal income tax.

It must be added that later publications of Knoester (1993, 1994 and 1995) found that in the US, the UK, Germany, France and the Netherlands the net effect of an equal cut in both government spending and direct taxation, including social security contributions, reduced unemployment – that is, that the stimulatory effect of the cuts in direct taxation outweighed the upward effect on unemployment of the reduction in government spending. Those later simulations do not give the effects of each of the two measures separately. Unlike the OECD simulations reported in Table 4.1, they appear to relate to public sector spending generally (not merely to non-wage expenditures); but, like the OECD simulation, they too relate to a range of direct taxation. Taken together with other simulations reported earlier which use personal income tax cuts only, this comparison suggests that it is likely that it is direct taxation *other than* personal income tax – presumably mainly employers' social security contributions and other taxes on employment (payroll taxes in the US and employers' national insurance contributions in the UK), and perhaps also taxation of corporations that have a greater effect on unemployment than does government spending.

Table 4.6: Simulated effects on unemployment rate in Germany, the Netherlands, the UK and the US of a simultaneous equal rise in both government spending and direct taxation
(%ge points change for a change in both fiscal measures equal to 1% of GDP in the same year)

	Germany		Netherlands		UK		US	
Year:	1	5	1	5	1	5	1	5
	0.1	1.5	0.1	1.2	0.7	0.8	–0.2	1.6

Source: Knoester (1983).

This last conclusion is supported by evidence that can be drawn from an EEC simulation in the mid-1980s, results of which are shown in Table 4.7.

It may be seen from Table 4.7 that, over the whole five years, by far the greatest effect in reducing unemployment (for a given rise in the budget deficit) of these four measures was from cuts in employers' social security contributions, followed by cuts in indirect taxation. Increases in public consumption are, on this evidence, only marginally more expansionary in terms of their effects in reducing unemployment than are cuts in income tax paid by households, which have the least effect of the four measures simulated. Again, coupled with the results reported in Table 4.1, this constitutes evidence that it is direct taxation other than personal income tax that has an appreciably larger effect on employment than changes in government non-wage outlays.

Table 4.7: Simulated effects on average unemployment rate in the EEC of various fiscal measures
(%ge points change for an average rise in the budget deficit equal to 1% of GDP over the same period)

Cut in employers' social security contributions	−1.72
Cut in indirect taxation (VAT)	−1.12
Rise in public consumption	−0.31
Cut in household direct taxation	−0.30

Source: Derived from Dramais (1986).

It may also be illuminating to relate these results to the change in the government's financial balance in the first year, as discussion of changes in the budget balance usually focuses on its changes in the year the policy changes are made.

It may be seen from Table 4.8 that in the first year or the first two years after the change, rises in government consumption have the greatest effect of these four measures in reducing unemployment, followed by cuts in indirect taxation. But for the fifth year (here considered in relation to the rise in the budget deficit in the first year), of these four fiscal measures the most expansionary in terms of reducing unemployment is a cut in employers' social security contributions, followed by cuts in indirect taxation; and that government consumption has by year 5 come to have the same effect as cuts in income tax.

If, therefore, public discussion is focused on the rise in government outlays and in the budget deficit in the first year, these results (shown in Table 4.8) suggest that a relatively large fall in unemployment may be brought about by rises in government consumption in the first two years, but at the expense of a much smaller fall in unemployment over the five years than could have been brought about by cuts in indirect taxation or cuts in employers' social security contributions having the same effect on the budget deficit in the first year. This implies that judging a budget on the basis of its first-year effects

on the government deficit may not give a good idea of its effects in relation
to the change in the budget deficit over several years.

Table 4.8: Simulated effects on unemployment rate in the EEC for
a 1% of GDP rise in the budget deficit in first year
(%ge points change in unemployment)

	Year 1	Years 1 and 2	Years 1–5
Employers' social security contributions	–0.11	–0.37	–4.78
Cuts in indirect taxation	–0.22	–0.35	–4.00
Rise in government consumption	–0.33	–0.44	–1.22
Cuts in household direct taxation	–0.11	–0.18	–1.22

Source: Derived from Dramais (1986).

EVIDENCE FOR THE US

It may be seen from Table 4.9 that the greatest effect on employment in the
US for a given effect on the budget deficit is obtained by a cut in indirect
taxation, followed by investment tax credits and labour tax credits. Cuts in
corporation tax and income taxation (in the form simulated here – which is
concentrated on higher income groups) have less upward effect on employment
than those measures for a given effect on the budget balance. The two forms
of government expenditure simulated here have the least effect on employment
for a given effect on the budget deficit. The relatively large effect on
employment of a labour tax credit and a value-added tax is consistent with
the similarly large effects for changes in VAT and in employers' social security
contributions (a tax on employment) in the EEC shown in Tables 4.7 and 4.8.

These simulations show that a cut in indirect taxation (signs reversed from
the original simulation, which was for an introduction of VAT), and also the
various forms of tax credit to businesses, especially a permanent labour tax
credit, provide a considerably greater stimulus to employment over the first
five years than does either government infrastructure investment or 'other'
(termed 'military') government spending (again, signs reversed from the
original simulation, which was for a cut in military spending). This ranking
differs somewhat from the ranking shown in Table 3.7 for the effects of these
various instruments on real output. In particular, to judge from the results
in Table 4.9, whereas a change in indirect tax has the greatest effect on
employment, followed by a permanent labour tax credit and both forms of

investment tax credit, in their relative effects on real output a permanent investment tax credit ranked above those tax credit measures. A cut in corporation tax ranked above either of the government spending measures simulated in terms of its effects on real GDP, but about the same as a gradual rise in government infrastructure investment in respect of its effect on employment.

Table 4.9: Simulated effects on employment in the US of various fiscal measures for a 1% of GDP change in the budget deficit
(Five-year total of %ge deviation of employment from baseline)

Cut in value-added tax	2.75
Permanent labour tax credit	2.19
Permanent investment tax credit	1.86
Temporary investment tax credit	1.16
Temporary labour tax credit	1.36
Government infrastructure investment (gradual)	0.66
Corporation tax cut	0.65
Non-investment government expenditure*	0.52
	(0.53)
Income tax cut	0.53
Lump-sum transfers to households	0.48
Government infrastructure investment (cut-off)	0.17

* See note to Table 3.7.

Source: Derived from graphical data in McKibbin and Bagnoli (1993) and numerical data supplied by the authors.

The simulation from which the results in Table 4.5 were derived suggested that, in the US, public spending reduces unemployment more than does a cut in direct taxation, in both years 1 and 5. This would seem to be consistent with the effects of a gradual rise in public investment simulated in McKibbin and Bagnoli by comparison with those of a cut in corporation tax or income tax.

A different simulation reported in Table 4.12 suggests that in the US a cut in direct taxation or a rise in public spending actually increased unemployment by the fifth year after the change.

Further results of this other simulation, drawn upon in Table 4.13, suggest that a cut in direct taxation reduces unemployment in the US by more than does a rise in public investment in both the first and the fifth year. This does not seem to be consistent with the ranking of income tax and corporation tax relative to a once-for-all ('cut-off') public infrastructure investment in the McKibbin and Bagnoli simulation; for changes in corporation tax in their simulations appear to have a greater effect on employment than most of the forms of government outlay simulated; but it should be borne in mind that in those simulations the form of income tax change simulated is one that has most of its effects on higher income groups, and would therefore be likely to have less effect than a general cut in income tax.

EVIDENCE FOR THE UK

For the two forms of fiscal stimulus for which a simulation for the UK is available published in 1995, as Table 4.10 shows, in three of the five models a cut in income tax has a bigger downward effect on unemployment than does a rise in government outlays of the same order (taking the total effect over the years 1, 3 & 5).

Table 4.10: Simulated effects on unemployment over five years of various fiscal measures in the UK
(Thousands, for a billion pounds rise in PSBR)

	LBS	NIESR*	HMT	OEF	COMPACT*
Rise in government outlays	−51.0	−159.4	−19.9	−30.6	−154.1
Income tax cut	-88.6	−89.9	−24.6	−41.7	−62.5

The simulation used is that with the fiscal solvency rule suppressed.
For source and key to models, see Table 3.8.
*In the NIESR model, both a rise in government expenditure and an income tax cut reduce the PSBR. The figures shown for that model are for the reduction in unemployment for a given *fall* in the PSBR. For the simulation with the COMPACT model, the rise in government spending reduces the PSBR over the period, whereas the income tax cut increases it. The figures for government outlays in that simulation thus show the reduction in unemployment associated with a given *fall* in the PSBR, and that for an income tax cut show the reduction in unemployment for a given *rise* in the PSBR.
In LBS, OEF and HMT models the PSBR change is the absolute difference (in billion pounds at 1990 prices). For NIESR it is the %ge point deviation of the ratio of the PSBR to GDP; and for COMPACT it is the percentage point deviation of the debt/GDP ratio. The figures in the table are therefore not comparable across all models.

In four models however, an income tax cut raises employment over the five years less than does a rise in government expenditure for a given effect on the PSBR. (See Table 6.11)

Some of this evidence suggests that the association in the public mind of expansionary fiscal measures with an increased deficit may be the opposite of the truth – at least in respect of certain fiscal measures; and that combinations of government outlays and income tax cuts could be found that would reduce unemployment while also reducing the PSBR, and that there are combinations of them that would reduce the PSBR while also reducing unemployment. These results appear to be inconclusive as to the relative effects of these two measures on unemployment in the UK; but on the balance of this inconclusive evidence, the effect of an income tax cut on employment appears likely to be smaller than that of a rise in government outlays. The balance of the evidence from the corresponding table for the ranking of their respective effects on real GDP (Table 3.6) suggested that government outlays had the greater relative effect of the two.

Although these results appear to be so diverse – and, indeed, mutually inconsistent in some respects – that it would be unwise to draw firm conclusions from them, it is clear that they imply that, for a given change in the PSBR, it makes a considerable difference whether one cuts income tax or raises government spending. For some models the PSBR actually falls after a rise in government expenditure; while for one model real GDP falls over the five years as a whole in response to an income tax cut.

Table 4.12 shows some earlier results for the UK, which include simulations of changes in indirect taxation and in employers' national insurance contributions, as well as for changes in government expenditure and income tax.

Table 4.11: Simulated effects on employment in the UK over five years of government expenditure and income tax cuts for a 1% of GDP rise in the PSBR in the first year
(Thousands)

Model:	LBS	NIESR*	HMT	OEF	COMPACT*
Income tax cut	0.33	0.31*	0.10	0.28	7.0*
Rise in gov't spending*	0.02	0.46*	0.31	0.94	26.9*

The simulation used is that with the fiscal solvency rule suppressed.
For source and key to models, see Table 3.8.
*In the NIESR model, both a rise in government expenditure and an income tax cut *reduce* the PSBR (expressed in that model as a percentage point deviation from trend in the ratio of the PSBR to GDP). The figures shown for that model are for the rise in real GDP for a given *fall* in the PSBR. For the simulation with the COMPACT model, the rise in government spending reduces the PSBR (expressed in the model in terms of the deterioration of the debt/GDP ratio over the period), whereas the income tax cut increases it. The figures for government outlays in that simulation thus show the rise in real GDP associated with a given *fall* in the PSBR, and that for an income tax cut show the reduction in GDP for a given *rise* in the PSBR.

*Table 4.12: Simulated effects on unemployment rate in
the UK of various fiscal measures*
(%ge points average change for a billion pounds rise in PSBR,
over five-year period)

Model:	LBS	NIESR	HMT	BE	OEF	STR
Rise in government spending	−0.13	−0.06	−0.05	−0.25	−0.13	−0.03
Income tax cut	−0.01	−0.03	−0.03	−0.03	−0.19	−0.09
Cut in VAT	−0.01	−0.03	−0.05	−0.08	−0.13	−0.04
Cut in employers' national insurance contributions	−0.02	−0.02	−0.06	−0.06	−0.06	−0.04

For key to models see Table 3.9.

Source: Derived from Church et al. (1993).

For four of the models, over the five-year period government expenditure has a bigger downward effect on unemployment (for a given rise in the PSBR) than do income tax cuts (at any rate, in the form simulated); and in three of them its downward effect on unemployment over the period is greater than that of any of the tax cuts simulated. But in one model, cuts in employers' national insurance contributions have a greater effect in reducing unemployment; while in each of the other two, either a cut in VAT or an income tax cut has a bigger effect than a rise in government outlays. In one model, all three forms of tax cut have a bigger downward effect on unemployment than the rise in government expenditure.

The simulation for three major countries reported in Table 4.13 suggests that a balanced budget increase that consists of the financing of government spending (in general) by increases in direct taxation (including social security contributions and other taxes on wages) may be expected to increase unemployment by the fifth year, or at best (in the case of the US) leave no net effect on it. But it also suggests that in the first year, at least, such a balanced budget increase is likely to reduce unemployment in Germany and the UK. As figures for intermediate years are not given, it is not possible to say from these results what the net effect on unemployment would be over the full five years. For the US, a rise in direct taxation alone appears to reduce unemployment by the fifth year.

Table 4.14 shows that if it is government investment that rises, financed by a rise in direct taxation (including social security contributions), the net effect on unemployment is for all four countries initially downwards, though sometime between the first and the fifth year that effect reverses, except for the US, where there continues to be a net downward effect on unemployment. One cannot from these figures say what the relative effects would be over the whole five-year period.

*Table 4.13: Simulated effects on unemployment rate of certain
fiscal measures in three major countries*
(%ge points change for an increase in public sector deficit equal
to 1% of GDP in the same year)

	Germany		UK		US	
	Year 1	Year 5	Year 1	Year 5	Year 1	Year 5
Rise in public spending	–0.2	0.7	–0.5	–0.5	–1.0	1.7
Rise in public spending and direct taxes	0.1	1.5	0.7	0.8	–0.2	0.0
Rise in direct taxes	0.3	0.8	1.2	1.3	0.8	–1.7

The figure for a rise in direct tax is derived as a residual from the other figures.
Note: The figure for government spending alone is stated as being financed by
borrowing in the capital market; the upward effect on unemployment in Year 5 for
Germany and the US is thus presumably due to 'crowding out' of private expenditure
to an extent that exceeds the stimulus from the government spending itself. The direct
taxes include taxes on wages and social security contributions, the simulation used
being that which takes account of the forward shifting of taxes into wages.

Source: Derived from Knoester (1983).

This result contrasts with the figures for the effect on the volume of output
given by the same simulation (reported in Chapter 3), where the net effect
on the volume of production is positive in the first year, and also in the fifth
year for the US, but becomes negative by year 5 for the three other countries.
For the US, therefore, there is no conflict in these figures between short-term
and medium-term objectives, nor as between the volume of production and
the level of unemployment as an objective: a rise in public investment
financed by an equal rise in direct taxation could be expected to reduce
unemployment and raise output. By the same token, therefore, a fall in the
budget deficit that consisted of a rise in direct taxation accompanied by a
somewhat smaller rise in public *investment* could therefore also be expected
to stimulate output and to reduce unemployment (while also reducing the
budget deficit). But if one considers the general level of all forms of
government spending, an equal cut in both direct taxation and government
spending could be expected to stimulate output and reduce unemployment
both in year 1 and (especially) in year 5 in all four countries. (See Table 8
in Knoester, 1995.) By the same token, therefore, a *shift* from public
consumption to public investment – even one that would involve some fall
in the budget deficit – could be expected to reduce unemployment and to
stimulate output in all four countries.

Table 4.14: Simulated effects on %ge unemployment rate in four countries of a rise equal to 1% of GDP in public investment and in direct taxation including social security contributions

Country:	Germany		Netherlands		UK		US	
Year	1	5	1	5	1	5	1	5
	−0.2	0.8	−0.1	0	−0.1	0.9	−0.6	−1.0

Source: Knoester (1995).

EVIDENCE FOR SOME SMALLER COUNTRIES

Evidence for Four Nordic Countries

It may be seen from Table 4.15 that for three of the four Nordic countries and four of the five models (two of the models being for Finland), over a five-year period, a rise in government spending on employment has a greater effect in reducing unemployment than does a cut in local income tax or in VAT. But in one model cuts in local income tax are the most effective of the three measures in reducing unemployment. The evidence for the ranking (and relatively greater effect) of government employment expenditure having the most significant effect on unemployment is clearly greater even than that for its ranking in terms of its effect on output (discussed in Chapter 3). It should, however, be borne in mind that (in contrast to other tables) the form of government spending simulated here is that on employment only.

Table 4.15: Simulated effects on unemployment of various fiscal measures in four Nordic countries
(Totals for years 1, 2, 3 & 5 of %ge deviation from baseline of unemployment for a given deviation from baseline in general government financial balance as a % of GDP)

Model:	ADAM	MODAG	KOSMOS	KESSU	BOF4
Rise in government employment	−2.28	−3.37	−2.42	−1.55	−0.45
Cut in VAT	−1.95	−0.07	−0.24	−0.46	−1.59
Cut in local income tax	−2.31	−0.03	−0.02	−0.06	−0.59

For key to models, see Table 3.12.
Note: It has been confirmed by the authors that the results they give for the simulation for local income tax are in fact for a reduction (whereas the table in the original states that it is for an increase). The signs in this table are those appropriate to a reduction.

Source: Derived from Wallis and Whitley (1991).

In Table 4.16 government employment outlays are seen also to have a greater effect on employment than either of the other two measures simulated in four of the five models, and in all models a cut in local income tax has a greater effect on employment than a cut in VAT.

*Table 4.16: Simulated effects on employment of various fiscal measures
in Nordic countries*
(Totals for Years 1, 2, 3 & 5 of %ge deviation from baseline of
employment for a given deviation from baseline in general government
financial balance as a % of GDP)

Model:	ADAM	MODAG	KOSMOS	KESSU	BOF4
Rise in government employment expenditure	2.49	8.36	6.49	1.79	1.23
Cut in local income tax	2.54	0.35	0.80	0.77	1.58
Cut in VAT	2.14	0.25	0.63	0.58	0.37

For key to models, see Table 3.12.

Source: Derived from Wallis and Whitley (1991).

Evidence for Belgium

The evidence in Table 4.17 for Belgium suggests that the measure with the greatest effect in reducing unemployment is a cut in VAT, followed by a cut in employers' social security contributions and then by employment in the public sector. Increases in state investment and in social security transfers, as well as cuts in income tax, have relatively little effect in reducing the level of unemployment over the five years. A comparison with Table 3.11, showing the relative effects of these measures on real GDP, indicates that public investment scores much more highly on that count than in terms of its ability to reduce unemployment; and that a cut in VAT ranks much higher in terms of its effect on employment and unemployment than it does in terms of its effect on real GDP.

Conclusions similar to those relating to effects on unemployment can be drawn from Table 4.18 for effects on employment, except that a cut in VAT had the greatest effect on unemployment, whereas public employment expenditure had the greatest effect in stimulating employment (as also in raising real GDP, as shown in Table 3.13).

It may be seen from Table 4.18 that changes in employment in the public sector had the greatest effect on employment, followed by a cut in VAT (which were also the two measures with the greatest effect on unemployment, but in the reverse order), and then employers' social security contributions. State investment and social security transfers have a much smaller effect on employment (as they did on unemployment), than on real GDP, with cuts in personal income tax having a still smaller effect (again, as in the table for unemployment). As with the results of these measures in terms of their relative effect on GDP (shown in Table 3.11), the results in Tables 4.17 and 4.18 are shown in the order of their effects on employment or unemployment. It may thus be seen that if the aim is to raise employment, or to cut unemployment, rather than primarily to raise real GDP, it would be preferable to reduce employers' social security contributions, as well as VAT, or to raise public sector employment, rather than to concentrate on raising state investment or increasing social security transfers to households, or to cut income tax – provided, of course, that the government also has the aim of keeping down the budget deficit.

Table 4.17: Simulated effects of various fiscal measures on percentage rate of unemployment for a change in the public sector deficit equal to 1% of GDP for Belgium
(Five-year totals)

Cut in VAT	−14.56
Rise in total employment in the public sector	−14.23
Cut in employers' social security contributions	−13.30
Rise in state investment	−2.45
Rise in social security transfers to households	−2.09
Cut in personal income tax	−1.53

Source: Derived from Bogaert et al. (1990).

These results may be consistent with those reported above relating to the OECD as a whole (Table 4.1), which related to *non-wage* government expenditures (which may be expected to have appreciably less effect on employment and unemployment than government expenditures on employment, or even public investment projects). Social security transfers are a major item in government non-wage expenditures, and the relatively low ranking of these in Tables 4.17 and 4.18 is consistent with the OECD finding for the area as a whole that non-wage expenditures have a relatively small effect on employment or unemployment.

*Table 4.18: Simulated effects of various fiscal measures
on employment in Belgium*
(Total percentage change from baseline relative to deviation of public sector
deficit from baseline as % of GDP over five years)

Rise in total employment in the public sector	1.42
Cut in VAT	1.33
Cut in employers' social security contributions	1.22
Rise in state investment	0.22
Rise in social security transfers to households	0.19
Cut in personal income tax	0.14

Source: Derived from Bogaert et al. (1990).

As we saw above, the OECD found (Tables 4.1 and 4.2) that a package of direct taxation changes have a large effect (relative to government non-wage outlays) on employment and unemployment. The figures for the effects of income tax cuts in Belgium imply that these are not the form of direct taxation that has the major effect on employment or unemployment. Presumably the effect of direct taxation found by the OECD would have resulted mainly from social security contributions (though taxation of companies, for which the evidence is not available from any of the simulations apart from the US, could also have been of importance). Perhaps in Belgium, a small open economy, an especially large proportion of increases in disposable income resulting from income tax cuts and social security transfers to households leaks away to other countries in the form of imports of goods and services.

Evidence for the Netherlands

It appears from Table 4.19 that, for the Netherlands, by year 5 the effect on the level of unemployment of a rise in direct taxation is less than that of a change in government spending.

Evidence for Portugal

A simulation for Portugal, results of which are shown in Table 4.20, shows that, of the measures tested, expenditure on public sector *employment*, followed by cuts in VAT, have the greatest effect in reducing unemployment; with public investment, followed by income tax cuts, having the least effect of these measures for a given change in the public sector deficit – a result that closely parallels that which we found for Belgium, another small country, in Table 4.17.

Table 4.19: Simulated effects on unemployment of various fiscal measures in the Netherlands
(%ge effect on employment of changes in various fiscal measures, each equal to 1% of GDP)

Cut in direct tax		Rise in public spending		Rise in direct tax & public spending	
Year 1	Year 5	Year 1	Year 5	Year 1	Year 5
−0.2	−0.5	−0.1	0.7	0.1	1.2

The figure for a cut in direct tax is derived as a residual from the other figures.

Source: Derived from Knoester (1983).

It may be seen from Table 4.20 that, of the four measures simulated for Portugal, the effect on *unemployment* in the year after the change is greatest for public sector employment, followed by cuts in direct taxation. Public investment has a considerably smaller effect, and cuts in indirect taxation still less (though to judge from the effects on consumption of cuts in direct taxation, the effect of this measure upon unemployment builds up fairly sharply over the subsequent years).

Table 4.20: Simulated effects on unemployment of various fiscal measures in Portugal
(%ge change for a given change in public borrowing as a percentage of GDP)

	Year after change	15 years after change
Rise in public sector employment	−1.28	−1.25
Cut in indirect taxation	−0.38	−0.64
Rise in public investment	−0.23	−1.16
Cut in direct taxation	−0.06	−0.25

Note that the figures are provided only for the first and fifteenth years.

Source: Derived from Modesto and Neves (1995).

Again, a comparison may be made with the simulation in Table 4.1 for the whole of OECD of changes in government non-wage expenditure and in direct taxation. It is clear that government expenditures that included employment have a much bigger effect than non-wage expenditures (which would constitute part of the figures in a number of tables for public investment). The small size of the effect of income tax cuts can be reconciled with the large effect of direct tax changes for the whole OECD; partly by the fact that a wider range of direct taxation is included in the simulation for the whole of the OECD; partly by the fact that the effects of a direct tax cut take some time to build up; and partly by the fact that as Portugal is a small economy, a relatively large part of the stimulatory effect of tax cuts (compared with those covering the whole of the OECD, and also by comparison with government spending on investment and employment) would presumably leak away towards imports.

A comparison with Table 3.15 showing the effects of these instruments upon real GDP in Portugal shows that indirect tax cuts ranked below the two forms of public outlay simulated in terms of their respective effects on real GDP (though above them in terms of the effect on unemployment).

CONCLUSIONS

Table 4.21: Ranking of effects on employment or unemployment of various fiscal measures simulated
(The most expansionary in terms of effects on employment or unemployment, or both, for a given effect on the budget balance, over the five years after the change, at the top of the table)

1   Public employment expenditures
2   Cuts in indirect taxation
3   Cuts in employers' social security or national insurance contributions
4   Public investment
5   Labour tax credit
6   Investment tax credit
7   Cut in corporation or company tax
8   Government consumption
9   Social security transfers
10 Income tax cuts
11 Government non-wage expenditure

As with the corresponding table at the end of Chapter 3, it must be emphasised that the exact order varies to some extent from country to country, and from model to model. The ranking given above is thus to some extent judgemental on the basis of the balance of the evidence considered. In general, however, it may be said that public sector employment and cuts in indirect taxation (VAT in most cases) rank higher in terms of their labour market effects than they were seen to in terms of their effects on real GDP. Morever, in the shorter run – of one to three years – government spending, especially employment expenditures, appear to have an especially marked effect on employment and unemployment.

5   Effects on Inflation

In deciding on its macroeconomic measures, a government cannot reasonably consider only the relative effects of different measures on output and employment (or unemployment). Some account of the relative effects on inflation has to be taken, even though the prevailing rates of inflation have been much lower in recent years than over the preceding two or three decades, if only because of the risk of bringing about a recrudescence of high rates of inflation.

A recent simulation for the OECD countries as a whole (using the OECD's Interlink model) of the relative effects on inflation of government non-wage expenditure and of changes in a range of direct taxation was published by the OECD in 1994 (Richardson et al., 1994).

It is clear from Table 5.1 that, on the evidence from this simulation, government non-wage expenditures had a greater upward effect on inflation for the total of the five years after the change than the package of direct tax *cuts* simulated and also had an upward effect on inflation in the fifth year – when government non-wage expenditure still had an effect much in excess of that of cuts in direct taxation.

Table 5.1: Simulated effects on average rate of increase in GDP price index for OECD over five years of a rise in government non-wage expenditure and cuts in direct taxation, with an accommodating monetary policy
(%ge points change in rate of increase for a rise in government net borrowing equal to 1% of GDP over five years)

	Five-year average	Effect in year 5
Rise in government non-wage expenditures	+0.89	+1.00
Cut in direct taxation	+0.36	+0.57

The simulation is that assuming unchanged real interest rates – that is, an accommodating monetary policy.

The original simulation is for a *cut* in government non-wage expenditure and a *rise* in a package of direct taxation. The signs are therefore the opposite to those shown in the original source table. The five years used are those beginning in the third year simulated, as no increase in government borrowing is assumed in this scenario for the first two years. The effect in the fifth year is related in the table to the change in government borrowing in that year.

Source: Derived from Richardson et al. (1994).

Table 5.2 suggests that with a non-accommodating monetary policy both groups of measures would tend to reduce inflation, but that direct tax cuts would do so to a greater extent than increases in government non-wage expenditure, which would increase in inflation by year 5.

Table 5.2: Simulated effects on inflation in the OECD over five years of government non-wage expenditures and direct tax cuts with non-accommodating monetary policy
(Average percentage point change for a rise in government net borrowing equal to 1% of GDP over five years, five-year total and effect in Year 5)

	Five-year total	Effect in Year 5
Government non-wage expenditures	−0.09	+0.19
Cut in direct taxation	−0.49	−0.16

The simulation assumes a low growth rate and a non-accommodating monetary policy.

The original simulation is for a *cut* in government non-wage expenditure and a *rise* in a package of direct taxation (and therefore assumes lower real interest rates). The signs are therefore the opposite to those shown in the original source.

The effect in the fifth year is related in the table to the change in government borrowing in that year.

Note: the simulation used here is that which assumes that the expansionary fiscal measure is in each case allowed to have its natural effect in raising real interest rates.

Source: Derived from Leibfritz et al. (1994).

Again, cuts in direct taxation were clearly superior to rises in government outlays (for the same effect on government net lending or borrowing) if the aim is to provide a stimulus with the least upward (or greatest downward) effect on inflation. If the over-riding aim was to cut the budget deficit, a reduction in government non-wage outlays did so with a relatively large reduction in inflation, whereas if this combination of direct taxes is increased, with the same effect in reducing the budget deficit, this would therefore reduce inflation by less.

An earlier simulation by the OECD (also with its Interlink model) for the seven major OECD countries, results derived from which are shown in Table 5.3, suggests that, with a constant money supply (that is, a non-accommodating monetary policy), for each of these seven countries except Canada government non-wage expenditures increased prices (the GDP price index) to a greater extent than did income tax cuts over the five years simulated. Tax cuts were clearly superior to government outlays on this score – so long as one aim is to hold down inflation while taking expansionary fiscal action.

Table 5.3: Simulated effects on average GNP/GDP price index over five years of government non-wage expenditures and personal income tax cuts for seven major OECD countries
(Percentage point change in index for a rise of in government financial balance equal to 1% of GDP)

	Rise in government non-wage expenditure	Cut in personal income tax
US	1.33	1.13
Japan	0.37	0.30
Germany	0.25	0.20
France	0.14	0.10
UK	0.18	0.09
Italy	0.20	0.16
Canada	0.75	0.49

The simulation used is that assuming a fixed money supply (a non-accommodating monetary policy) and floating exchange rates.

Source: Figures for effects of government expenditures derived from Richardson (1987); figures for effects of personal income tax cuts kindly supplied by that author on the basis of analogous simulations completed at the same time as those for government expenditures.

If cuts in employers' social security contributions are likely to reduce inflation (or, at least, less likely to increase inflation than are cuts in household income taxes), cuts in a range of direct taxes that included employers' social security contributions would be less likely to increase inflation (or more likely to reduce it) than cuts in personal income tax rates alone. It may be seen that in Table 5.3 (which assumes a fixed money supply – in that sense a non-accommodating monetary policy) personal income tax cuts do increase inflation in each country; whereas in the later simulations for the whole of the OECD, using a package of tax measures and a non-accommodating monetary policy (in the sense that real interest rates are allowed to rise), the tax cuts in question actually reduced inflation.

Simulations undertaken with a number of different country models (including two different models for Canada) in response to questionnaires from the OECD published in 1984, results of which are shown in Table 5.4, also suggest that for the seven major countries (except for one of the two models for Canada), real non-wage government expenditure had a greater upward effect on the average price level over the years simulated than did cuts in personal income tax. But for the other model for Canada, and for Australia, personal income tax cuts had the greater upward effect on the price level. For the major countries these results are consistent with those indicated in Table 5.3 (and also for the OECD as a whole in Tables 5.1 and 5.2).

Table 5.4: Simulated effects on GDP/GNP price index of various countries of government non-wage expenditures and personal income tax cuts
(Percentage point change for a change in government borrowing in the first year equal to 1% of GDP/GNP, average of Years 1, 2, 3 & 7 after the change)

	Real government expenditure	Cut in income tax
US	0.52	0.34
Japan	1.13	0.69
France	0.32	0.00
UK	1.17	0.35
Canada 1	0.61	0.59
Canada 2	0.50	0.69
Australia	1.68	2.91
Netherlands	1.25	1.07
New Zealand*	0.50	0.46

The simulation used is that with floating exchange rates and a non-accommodating monetary policy.
*Average of years 1, 3 & 5 only.

Source: Derived from Chan-Lee and Kato (1984).

SIMULATIONS FOR THE EEC

Simulations for the then EEC made in the mid-1980s by the EEC secretariat suggest that, for a given rise in the budget deficit, cuts in employers' social security contributions reduced the rate of inflation over the first five years as a whole, and still did so even during the fifth year – so that, clearly, this was not just a short-run impact effect. Cuts in indirect taxation also reduced inflation over the average of the first five years, but by the fifth year the rate of inflation was higher than without the cut in indirect taxes – though the *price level* remained lower than it would have been without them. Income tax cuts increased the rate of inflation over the five years as a whole and also in the fifth year. Government consumption expenditure raised inflation over the average of the five years; and in the fifth year, according these simulations, government consumption expenditure increased inflation to a greater extent than any of the tax cuts simulated. It seems, therefore, that a government wishing to provide a stimulus with a minimal upward effect on the budget deficit, and preferably with a downward effect on inflation, would cut employers' social security contributions, or indirect taxation, rather than raise household income tax or increase government consumption.

Table 5.5: Simulated effects on inflation in the EEC of various
fiscal measures over five years
(Average %ge rate of increase in GDP price index for a rise in the budget deficit averaging 1% of GDP over 5 years, with actual inflation rate in Year 5 in parentheses)

Cut in employers' social security contributions	–0.12	(–0.3)
Cut in household indirect taxation	–0.05	(0.3)
Cut in household direct taxation	0.05	(0.3)
Rise in public consumption	0.10	(0.4)

Source: Derived from Dramais (1986).

A government wishing to reduce the budget deficit would do better to curb government expenditures, or to raise income tax or even indirect taxation, than to raise employers' social security contributions. (These figures relate to the average *rate of inflation* over the period: if the criterion is the effect on the average *price level* over the period, it may be more relevant to observe that a cut in indirect taxation *reduced* the price level over the average of the five years, as did a cut in employers' national insurance contributions, whereas the other two measures *increased* the average price level.)

These results may be compared with those reported in Tables 5.1 and 5.2 for the effects of government non-wage expenditures and for changes in a range of direct taxation. It is not surprising that the simulation for the whole of the OECD found that government non-wage expenditures – which would include some outlays on public consumption – were more inflationary than were reductions in a range of direct taxation; for the EEC simulation suggests that cuts in employers' social security contributions (which were included in the OECD's package of direct taxation), or in indirect taxation or personal income tax, were less likely to raise (or more likely to reduce) prices than were increases in public consumption. Cuts in the first two forms of taxation (in contrast to cuts in income tax) tend, on these EEC results, to *reduce* the general price level.

Table 5.6 presents a somewhat similar picture, as, like the OECD simulation reported in Table 5.1, it relates to a package of direct tax cuts, but, unlike the OECD simulation, it relates to public spending in general. It is clear that these results suggest that public spending in general had a greater upward effect on inflation than a package of direct tax cuts, and that this is true for the US, Japan (except in year 5), and the European group of countries covered in the simulation (the EEC as it was in 1988).

*Table 5.6: Simulated effects on GDP price index of direct tax cuts
and public spending in the US, the UK and Europe*
(%ge change in Years 1 and 5 for a rise in the
budget deficit equal to 1% of GDP)

Year:	US		Japan		Europe	
	1	5	1	5	1	5
Direct tax cut	0.09	1.46	0.06	1.09	0.00	1.67
Rise in public spending	0.26	2.56	0.12	0.63	1.15	2.93

Source: Derived from Knoester (1988).

EVIDENCE FOR THE US

It may be seen from Table 5.7 that a reduction of indirect tax would have a downward effect on the rate of inflation, as would permanent investment tax credits and a permanent labour tax credit. Moreover, an indirect tax cut continued to reduce the rate of inflation on these simulations right up to the fifth year, so that it cannot be argued that this a merely a short-term, impact, effect. Cuts in income tax and rises in government infrastructure investment would, however, increase inflation. The surprising result for non-infrastructure government expenditure in this simulation, which on these results appears to reduce inflation over the five years after the change is announced (the figure shown in parentheses), seems to be a consequence of the pattern of changes in these expenditures over time that is assumed in the simulation – the measures being announced well before they are implemented. The main figure in the text is therefore for the five years beginning three years after the change is announced, which is when the implementation of these measures occurs and starts to have its direct effects.

A cut in income tax (in the form simulated – mainly towards higher income groups) had a slightly smaller upward effect on inflation than did government infrastructure investment, and somewhat less than that of non-investment government spending, which had less upward effect on inflation than other forms of government spending or any of the other measures that increase inflation; while a temporary labour tax credit and a temporary investment tax credit had the greatest upward effect on inflation of the measures simulated here (in relation to their effect on the budget deficit).

Government infrastructure expenditures tend to reduce inflation from the fifth year onwards, whereas the other forms of government spending tend to increase it in these later years (not shown in the table). (If the infrastructure investment has the effect of increasing the country's productivity over the period as a whole, one might expect it to reduce inflation in the long period.)

The relative effects on inflation of these tax measures simulated here for the US may thus be summarised as follows:

(i)   Cuts in indirect taxation would reduce inflation, as would permanent labour and investment tax credits.

(ii) A cut in income tax (in the form simulated here – which is predominantly for higher income groups) had a smaller upward effect on inflation than either form of government spending. Government infrastructure investment, corporation tax cuts and temporary tax credits for investment or labour increased inflation over the five years as a whole, but tended to reduce it in some later years.

The downward effect on inflation of both cuts in indirect taxation and permanent investment and labour tax cuts may help to explain their high ranking in terms of the stimulus they provide for employment and real GDP growth (shown in Tables 3.7 and 4.9).

Table 5.7: Simulated effects on inflation of various fiscal measures in the US for a given effect on the budget deficit
(Five-year total of percentage deviation from baseline of inflation for a given change in the budget deficit as % of GDP)

Cut in indirect taxation	−1.52
Lump-sum transfers to households	−0.24
Permanent labour tax credit	−0.28
Permanent investment tax credit	−0.21
Non-investment government spending*	+0.09 (−0.11)**
Corporation tax cut	+0.03
Income tax cut	+0.14
Government infrastructure investment (cut-off)	+0.19
Government infrastructure investment (gradual)	+0.18
Temporary labour tax credit	+0.75
Temporary investment tax credit	+0.89

* See note to Table 3.7.
** For an explanation see text.

Source: As for Table 3.7.

EVIDENCE FOR THE UK

In the UK, the average effect on inflation or the price level of government spending over the five years after the change of policy for a given effect on the budget balance (the PSBR) was, on the balance of the evidence drawn upon in Table 5.8, clearly greater than the effect of income tax cuts, to judge from the results from five of the six models shown (Strathclyde, the smallest model, being the exception).

Of the three tax changes simulated, the cut in income tax appears on this evidence the most likely to raise prices – or to raise them by more than any other tax cut – whereas the cut in employers' national insurance contributions reduced the average price level over the period in two of the models. But in the Bank of England model, income tax cuts reduced inflation over the period (though to a lesser extent than did the other tax cuts simulated).

Table 5.8 provides strong evidence that a cut in VAT was for the UK the form of tax cut most likely to reduce prices over the five-year period (for a given effect on the PSBR) and to reduce the rate of inflation. For in every model, the cut in VAT had a downward effect on the price level greater than any reduction attributable to other measures, except that in certain models the cut in employers' national insurance contributions had a slightly greater downward effect on the price level, or the rate of inflation, or both, than a cut in VAT; and in one model the cut in VAT raised prices slightly.

The evidence from these University of Warwick simulations, therefore, suggests that cuts in VAT and in national insurance contributions were likely to reduce inflation over the five years after the change, whereas income tax cuts were more likely to increase it, though probably to a smaller extent than government spending. This conclusion is consistent with that which can be drawn from the EEC simulations summarised in Table 5.5.

On balance, cuts in employers' national insurance contributions seem, on this evidence, more likely to exert downward pressure on the price level than do income tax cuts, though in simulations with the four models that show upward pressure on the price level resulting from cuts in employers' national insurance contributions, the effect is greater than that from income tax cuts in two of the models.

Results from a more recent simulation with five models are shown in Table 5.9. This evidence is not conclusive as to whether income tax cuts or government spending has the greater upward effect on the price level or inflation; but, on balance, it probably tends to confirm the view that income tax cuts are likely to have a smaller inflationary effect than a rise in government expenditure, or even a downward effect on the rate of inflation. Certainly, the balance of this evidence does not run counter to the conclusion on this point suggested by the earlier simulations reported in Table 5.8.

Table 5.8: Simulated effects of government expenditure and various tax cuts for the UK on the level and rate of increase in index of consumption prices for a billion pounds change in the PSBR
(%ge deviation of price level from baseline, five-year average; deviation of rate of inflation in parentheses)

	LBS	NIESR	HMT	BE*	OEF	STR	Average	Median
Government spending	0.88	1.43	0.44	4.43	1.07	0.65	1.48	0.97
	(0.43)	(0.41)	(0.17)	(2.06)	(0.52)	(0.19)	(0.63)	(0.42)
Cut in VAT	−0.53	0.45	−0.84	−1.32	−0.30	0.25	−0.38	−0.42
	(−0.19)	(0.19)	(−0.23)	(−0.29)	(−0.08)	(0.14)	(−0.08)	(−0.06)
Income tax cut	0.80	0.77	0.04	−0.08	0.12	1.80	0.57	0.45
	(0.08)	(0.26)	(0.01)	(0.02)	(0.03)	(0.54)	(0.16)	(0.15)
Cut in employers' national insurance contributions	0.26	0.80	−0.80	−0.60	−0.36	0.65	0.01	0.31
	(0.12)	(0.26)	(−0.26)	(0.23)	(−0.05)	(0.12)	(0.06)	(0.12)

*Four years only.
For key to models see Table 3.6.

Source: Derived from Church et al. (1993).

Table 5.9: Simulated effects on the price level in the UK of two fiscal measures
(%ge point change, with %ge point difference in the rate of inflation in parentheses. Average of Years 1, 3 & 5 per unit change in PSBR)

Model	LBS	NIESR*	HMT	OEF	COMPACT*
Income tax cut	0.07	0.77	−0.05	−0.56	2.12
	(−0.04)	(0.09)	(0.03)	(0.14)	(0.12)
Government spending	0.05	0.29	0.14	0.20	11.44
	(0.00)	(0.01)	(0.03)	(0.07)	(2.66)

The simulation for government expenditure is that with the fiscal solvency rule suppressed.
* In the NIESR model, both a rise in government expenditure and an income tax cut *reduce* the PSBR (expressed in that model as a percentage point deviation from trend in the ratio of the PSBR to GDP) in the first year. The figures shown for that model are for the rise in real GDP for a given *fall* in the PSBR in Year 1. For the simulation with the COMPACT model, the rise in government spending reduces the PSBR (expressed in the model in terms of the change in the debt/GDP ratio in Year 1), whereas the income tax cut increases it. The figures for government outlays in that simulation thus show the rise in real GDP associated with a given *fall* in the PSBR, and that for an income tax cut show the increase in GDP for a given *rise* in the PSBR.

Source: Derived from Church et al. (1995).

EVIDENCE FOR SOME SMALLER COUNTRIES

Evidence for Four Nordic Countries

It may be seen from Table 5.10 that, in the five Nordic country models used for these simulations, government employment expenditure has a consistently upward effect on the price level. Again, in all the models, cuts in VAT reduce the price level over the five years while cuts in local income tax increase it, but usually by less than government employment expenditure.

Table 5.10: Simulated effects on average price level of various fiscal measures in four Nordic countries, average of years 1, 2, 3 & 5
(%ge deviation from baseline of price level for a given deviation
from baseline in general government financial balance as a % of GDP)

Model:	ADAM	MODAG	KOSMOS	KESSU	BOF4
Government employment expenditure	2.40	0.83	4.71	0.00	0.51
Cut in local income tax	1.75	0.41	0.70	0.00	1.29
Cut in VAT	−5.73	−2.29	−3.54	−2.29	−0.13

For key to models, see Table 3.12.
Note: It has been confirmed by the authors that the results they give for the simulation for local income tax are in fact for a *reduction* (whereas the table in the original states that it is for an *increase*). The signs in this table are those appropriate to a reduction.

Source: Derived from Wallis and Whitley (1991).

Table 5.11: Simulated effects on the rate of inflation in Year 5 of various fiscal measures in four Nordic countries
(Deviation from baseline of inflation in Year 5 for a given deviation from baseline in general government financial balance in that year as a % of GDP)

Model:	ADAM	MODAG	KOSMOS	KESSU	BOF4
Government expenditure	2.37	3.50	10.00	0.01	0.94
Cut in local income tax	1.00	−0.65	1.30	0.00	3.00
Cut in VAT	−3.90	−2.45	−2.82	−1.69	−1.10

For key to models, see Table 3.12.

Source: Derived from Wallis and Whitley (1991).

Evidence for Belgium

It may be seen from Table 5.12, relating to Belgium, that public expenditure on employment in the public sector had a greater upward effect on inflation as measured by the annual rate of change in the private consumption deflator (or 'price index') than any of the other measures simulated; and that rises

Table 5.12: Simulated effects of various fiscal measures on
rate of inflation in Belgium
(Five-year average of percentage point change in private
consumption deflator for a fiscal measure equal to 1% of GDP)

Rise in total employment in the public sector	0.22
Rise in state investment	0.00
Rise in social security transfers to households	0.03
Cut in personal income tax	0.03
Cut in employers' social security contributions	0.08
Cut in VAT on consumption products	−0.32

Source: Derived from Bogaert et al. (1990).

in state investment had no appreciable upward effect on this measure of the annual rate of inflation. Cuts in personal income tax and rises in social security transfers to households had only a fairly small upward effect on inflation, but cuts in employers' social security contributions had an appreciably larger upward effect – in contrast to the results for the EEC as a whole shown in Table 5.6 and for labour tax credits in the US, shown in Table 5.7. One reason that may account for this difference is the much greater openness of the Belgian economy, and the likelihood that a high proportion of rises in post-tax incomes would be spent on imports compared with that spent within the country (and thus do less to raise domestic prices).

These results may be reconciled with the relative effects on inflation for the OECD as a whole of changes in government non-wage expenditures and changes in direct taxation summarised in Tables 5.1 and 5.2; for those tables showed that government non-wage expenditures had a greater upward effect on inflation than did cuts in a range of direct taxation. In the simulation for Belgium, as we have seen, the non-wage item of social security transfers had a more inflationary effect than either of the types of direct tax cut included in this simulation one being cuts in employers' social security contributions. But another item that would include non-wage expenditures, that is state investment, was not inflationary, whereas government expenditure on employment or income tax cuts increased inflation, as did also government expenditure on employment.

Evidence for Portugal

It may be seen from Table 5.13, relating to Portugal, that (as for Belgium) cuts in indirect taxation in Portugal have a downward effect on the price level over the average of the five years. Of the other three measures, the rise in public investment has by far the greatest upward effect on prices in the first year (though in later years one might expect that result to be reversed – to judge by the evidence from other models discussed above), followed by the rise in public sector employment, with income tax cuts having a smaller upward effect on consumer prices than those forms of government outlay.

Table 5.13: Simulated effects of various fiscal measures on level of consumer prices in Portugal
(Five-year average of percentage point change in consumer prices for a change in public borrowing equal to 1% of GDP)

Rise in public investment	1.70
Rise in public sector employment	1.29
Cut in household direct taxation	1.03
Cut in indirect taxation	−1.26

Source: These figures are only approximate, being derived from graphical data in Modesto and Neves (1995).

Table 5.14 gives results derived from graphical data in a simulation for Ireland. It shows both forms of public expenditure simulated as having an upward effect on consumer prices over the average of the five years following the change. For both expenditures, the extent of the upward effect on prices in the first two years is somewhat reversed in the next few years – though the price level remains well above what it was before the change in policy. A cut in indirect taxation has a substantial downward effect on consumer prices in the first year or two, and after the first year the rate of inflation is still reduced substantially.

Other small countries for which it appears from published simulations that a cut in indirect taxation exerts a downward effect on prices (generally for many years afterwards) – in contrast to all the other forms of fiscal expansion simulated – are those for Spain (Herce and Sosvilla-Rivero, 1995) and Israel (Beenstock et al., 1994). Indeed, the firmest conclusion that one can draw from these various simulations relating to inflation is that cuts in indirect taxation are the least inflationary form of stimulus (and most likely to reduce it over at least a five-year period), and that attempts to reduce the budget deficit by increasing indirect taxation will tend to make inflation worse (as well as having a greater downward effect on real output or employment than most alternative fiscal measures having the same effect on the budget balance).

Table 5.14: Simulated effects of certain fiscal measures on consumer price index for Ireland
(Five-year average of %ge change in consumer prices for rise in government borrowing equal to 1% of GDP)

Rise in public employment	0.71
Rise in public infrastructure investment	0.52
Cut in indirect tax	−1.60

Note: In the original source only multipliers are given for each year for the two forms of public outlay, and not the effect on the government borrowing in each year. For the indirect tax cut the figure shown is the change in prices over the five-year period for a 1% deviation from baseline of the level of government borrowing.

Source: Derived from graphical data in Bradley et al. (1995).

CONCLUSIONS

Table 5.15 shows a tentative ranking of the principal fiscal measures simulated in models drawn upon in tables in this chapter in terms of their effects in reducing or increasing the upward pressure on the price level or inflation. (The measures that may reduce inflation over the five-year period, or increase it least, are at the top of the list.) To some extent the ranking is judgemental on points of detail; but it is consistent with the overwhelming balance of the evidence drawn upon above.

Table 5.15: Ranking order of effects of various fiscal measures on inflation for a given change in the budget balance
(*Least* inflationary expansionary measure over five years at top)

1	Cuts in indirect taxation
2	Cuts in employers' social security or national insurance contributions
3	Labour tax credit
4	Investment tax credit
5	Cut in corporation or company tax
6	Income tax cuts
7	Public investment expenditure
8	Government consumption
9	Social security transfer payments
10	Government non-wage expenditure
11	Public employment expenditures

Note: Some of the classifications, especially those relating to government outlays, are overlapping, as a result of the varying definitions and sub-categories of government expenditure used in the different simulations.

In principle, if the aim is to reduce inflation, or to increase it as little as possible, and if the aim is to do this without increasing the budget deficit, this could be done by moving one of the instruments near the top of the table in the expansionary direction, while simultaneously moving one of the measures near the bottom of the table to an appropriate extent in a contractionary direction.

For example, cuts in employers' social security contributions or in indirect taxes would give a stimulus that would have a downward effect on inflation over the short and medium term, while cuts in most forms of government outlays, or increases in income tax, would be able to offset any undesired budgetary effects, while still leaving a net (non-inflationary) stimulus. If the aim is to reduce the level of government borrowing in a way that is likely also to reduce inflation, it would be best to restrain government outlays, rather than to increase indirect taxation or employers' social security contributions or income taxation.

Table 5.15 shows a very different ranking from that shown in Chapters 3 and 4 for the effects on output or employment and unemployment (for a given effect on the budget deficit). (Those tables are reproduced below for purposes of comparison with that for the effects on inflation.) The two measures most likely to reduce inflation rank below government investment expenditure or expenditure on employment in terms of their effect on real output or employment for a given effect on the budget deficit. But changes in government non-wage expenditure and in government consumption rank below cuts in income tax and social security transfers in terms of their effect on real output or employment, though they appear likely to be among the most inflationary measures simulated. These results emphasise the importance of not drawing conclusions about government outlays in general, or taxation in general, as may happen if one looks only at the effects of government non-wage expenditures and packages of various types of direct taxation (some types of which are much less likely to raise inflation, or likely to raise it by less, than are personal income tax cuts). It also emphasises the need to take account of the relative effects of the different measures upon *all* the macroeconomic objectives that are considered to be important.

If the aim is to provide a real stimulus without increasing the budget deficit, one of the measures near the top of the table should be changed in an expansionary direction, and any undesired effect on the budget balance offset by a contractionary movement of one of the measures near the bottom of the table. For instance, a rise in government investment expenditure or a cut in value-added tax might be combined with a reduction in govenment consumption or non-wage expenditure, or a rise in personal income tax.

Table 5.16: Ranking order of effects of various fiscal measures on real output for a given change in the budget balance
(Most expansionary over five years in terms of effect on real output at the top)

1	Rises in government expenditure on employment
2	Rises in government investment expenditure
3	Tax concessions for private investment
4	Labour tax credit
5	Cuts in value-added tax
6	Cuts in social security or national insurance contributions by employers
7	Cuts in company or corporation tax
8	Rises in government non-wage expenditure
9	Rises in government consumption
10	Rises in social security transfers
11	Cuts in personal income tax

If the aim is to reduce the budget deficit without reducing real output or increasing inflation, the appropriate combination of measures would therefore involve linking a contractionary movement of one of the measures nearer to the bottom of both tables with a movement of one of the measures near the top of both tables in an expansionary direction.

An example of such a combination might be a cut in value-added tax coupled with a rise in income tax or a reduction in government consumption expenditures. Some examples of combinations of measures that would reduce the budget deficit with a helpful effect in both holding down inflation and holding up real output will be considered in the final chapter.

Table 5.17: Ranking order of effects of various fiscal measures on employment or unemployment for a given change in the budget balance
(The most expansionary in terms of effects on employment or unemployment, or both, over the five years after the change at the top)

1	Public employment expenditures
2	Cuts in indirect taxation
3	Cuts in employers' social security or national insurance contributions
4	Public investment
5	Labour tax credit
6	Investment tax credit
7	Cut in corporation or company tax
8	Government consumption
9	Social security transfers
10	Income tax cuts
11	Government non-wage expenditure

6 Effects on National Net Wealth

A third possible macroeconomic objective (in addition to those of holding down inflation and holding up real output or employment) may be termed 'changes in the country's net wealth'. That is to say, changes in its stock of useful productive capital plus or minus its net liabilities owed to or assets held in other countries. It is reasonable for a government to include this as one macroeconomic objective, for it measures the contribution of policy to determining how much the present generation is handing on to future generations by way of a larger stock of productive capital, net of debts owed to other countries (or plus assets held in other countries).

Alternatively, it may take the form of the extent to which the present generation is in effect borrowing from future generations (or at least from itself in future years) by inflicting costs on the country in future in the form of a burden of higher taxation (to finance debts owed either within the country or outside it), or a lower level of useful productive capital than would otherwise be possible.

Another way of expressing this objective is to speak of national 'saving'; for a country can finance its investment either from its own saving or by borrowing from (or reducing net assets in) other countries.

It is important to bear in mind that an increase in the proportion of its income that a country decides to save will not automatically ensure that the increased flow of saving (for a given level of income) will become embodied in a higher level of productive investment. Indeed, a decision to save more out of a given income may in itself lead to a fall in the total level of income, and thus in the demand for finished products, and so also in the level of investment in capital goods to produce those finished products. Nor will a decision to save a higher proportion of a country's income necessarily lead to a strengthening of its current account balance (that is, a fall in the amount it is borrowing from other countries, or a rise in the amount it is lending to them). The country's 'total saving' may be substituted for the concept of its 'net wealth', provided this is not confused with the proportion of a given income that a country is saving, an increase in which, taken alone, can well reduce total income and thus total saving – and also productive investment.

Some have argued that decisions that affect the country's saving, investment and current account balance can and should be left to the market; whereas others would say that one important role of government is to act to some extent as a custodian of the interests of future generations (or, of course, those of the present generation in future years) – as the market may tend to take short-term views on these matters, discounting the future excessively. One might also argue that one role of a government should be to ensure that an excessive proportion of current income is not devoted to benefiting posterity – which may be expected to be a good deal wealthier than the current generation.

In any case, for the purposes of the present analysis it is sufficient to point out that the decisions of governments about their expenditure and taxation policies inevitably influence the country's stock of useful capital, the proportion of the country's income that is saved, the level of its current account surplus or deficit, and the amount of taxation required in future to service government debt. Sound policy involves taking a view about whether reductions in net wealth (or increases in it) in a given year are such as to put excessive or inadequate weight upon the welfare of future generations compared with the present one.

These inter-generational transfers are therefore matters that governments cannot avoid being concerned with. Indeed, the popular and political discussions of budget deficits and current account balances are directly concerned with such matters – though only to a partial extent. They are best regarded as implicitly being discussions about whether too much or too little net wealth is being handed on to future generations – inadequate though these two concepts are as a guide to the changes that occur in net wealth.

It is, however, very misleading, and potentially dangerous, to focus policy discussion upon the budget balance and the current account balance alone. For these are only partial approximations to what is really at stake – namely, the net burdens or benefits being passed on to future generations.

We have seen in Chapter 2 that focusing on the budget balance without considering the extent of the government's investment in human and material capital may lead governments to reduce the country's stock of capital by more than (or fail to build it up as much as) would be defensible in the light of some appropriate combination of the interests of future generations and those of the present generation.

In the same way, to focus on reducing the current account deficit in the balance of payments may well lead a government to take measures that cut back its own spending on useful productive assets, such as infrastructure (roads, schools and so on) and of investment in human capital, or, through its tax measures, have a downward effect on useful productive investment by the private sector. Discussions about what effects policy decisions should be aiming to have on budget balances or current account balances are by implication assuming that a reduction in the budget deficit or the current account deficit can be brought about without having any comparable adverse effects on the other items in the national balance sheet of net wealth.

But in fact macroeconomic policy decisions inevitably affect both investment in capital and the level of domestic saving available to finance it. Any measure to increase the government's saving through a higher budget surplus or lower budget deficit will almost inevitably have some greater or smaller adverse effect on the saving of the private sector, or on the level of useful productive investment by the private sector, or both. Those decisions may also, of course, affect public investment – in roads, schools, transport and human capital. The total effect on national net wealth will therefore be different from that on the budget balance or that on the current account balance. But both those indicators of changes in net wealth have some bearing on the outcome.

Some economists who have argued strongly that the current account balance should not be an objective of policy have failed to adopt instead this broader objective of national net wealth – perhaps partly in the fear or expectation that to do so would allow in by the back door discussions and policy decisions directed at the current account as such. There may well be some danger of this happening. But the way to deal with this problem is to emphasise constantly that the current account of the balance of payments is only one item in the national balance sheet; and that the budget balance is only one item affecting (in various ways according to the pattern of outlays and revenue) the level of the national stock of capital and the taxation burden to be inflicted on future generations. For example, future generations would not object to being saddled with a higher level of taxation if this was offset by having consequently bequeathed to them a sufficiently larger stock of useful productive capital (including human capital).

Though the arguments against making the current account an objective in itself (and taken by itself) are compelling, it has to be acknowledged that governments are likely to continue to consider the state of the country's current account balance as one of their objectives. In particular, so long as there is a widespread (however confused) view that the current account balance is important in itself, to that extent it is important for a government to take some account of it, as it will affect its popularity and electoral success – as well as its credibility in financial markets.

One should, however, urge governments not to try to improve the country's current account in ways that have an adverse effect on the country's net national wealth greater than whatever benefit is expected to result from 'improving' the current account balance. It is even more important that it should not be brought about by reducing the country's output and employment below the level that would otherwise have been found desirable and feasible; for the adverse welfare consequences of doing so are almost always likely to exceed whatever benefits may result from strengthening the current account balance.

At the same time, it must be acknowledged that a rising current account deficit is sometimes one indication that the country is permitting excess demand – a rise in demand greater than its capacity (including its capacity to finance economically the consequent level of imports). But if this is true, the excess demand should be tackled as such – quite apart from its effects on the current account balance.

So long as a policy-maker feels obliged to take account of the current account balance in itself, it will be de facto relevant to substitute the words 'strengthening of the current account' for the words 'increase in the country's net wealth' in the analysis that follows. (It is preferable to avoid the word 'improvement' in connection with the effect on the current account, as that word appears to pre-judge the question of whether there will be a net benefit to the country from reducing the current account deficit – or increasing the surplus. A good example of a case where the opposite may well have been true is that of Japan in the first half of the 1990s, and perhaps over a longer period, where the large current account surpluses caused problems for Japan and other countries, leading to appreciation of the yen and consequent falls in the profitability of many Japanese industries.)

SOME EFFECTS OF DIFFERENT FISCAL MEASURES ON THE CURRENT ACCOUNT BALANCE AND NET WEALTH

There are many ways in which a government's choice of fiscal instruments may affect the country's net wealth (and the current account balance as part of changes in that net wealth).

In the first place, the overall setting of a country's macroeconomic policy affects the general level of activity; and if the net effect of the government's policy is to reduce the growth of output and employment, although this will tend to strengthen the current account balance, it will reduce the rate of addition to the country's stock of useful productive capital.

It will also tend to reduce the rate at which human capital is trained for appropriate jobs; for if the jobs are not available the incentive for labour to move in the right directions, and to train to do work for which it is suited, will be weakened. There is a strong presumption that the country's economic welfare will be reduced by these effects to a greater extent than it may benefit from any strengthening of the current account that is brought about by deflating the level of demand to appreciably below that which would otherwise have been feasible.

The setting of fiscal instruments at any given level of employment or real output may also have effects on net wealth, including the state of the current account. In this connection it will always be more appropriate to prefer combinations of fiscal instruments that will tend to increase net wealth as well as strengthening the current account – rather than strengthening the current account alone. Policy measures that increase net wealth by affecting the allocation of resources at a given level of activity are always preferable to incurring the costs and losses resulting from reducing activity below what would have been feasible.

The first and most obvious way in which governments can use fiscal measures to affect net wealth and the current account balance is by their own expenditure. If a government attempts to improve the current account balance by reducing its own spending on useful infrastructure, the consequent decline in net wealth is likely to exceed whatever benefit arises from the stronger current account. If, however, the government reduces its expenditure overseas – on such items as defence or diplomatic activity – that will tend to strengthen the current account (and to that extent increase national net wealth) without reducing its outlays within the country, so that there is no general presumption that this form of reduction in government outlays will reduce the level of activity or domestic real investment.

Of course, if the government overseas expenditure that is cut would have been on items that would have enabled it to add to the country's stock of useful capital (even if located abroad), there would be no presumption that the 'improvement' in the country's balance of payments would increase the country's net wealth.

In general, government spending on productive capital (including human capital) in large and highly industrialised countries probably has a relatively low import content (apart from those forms of capital investment associated with overseas military spending). A reduction in the general level of government spending on goods and services will thus often tend to reduce domestic activity more than imports. (The United Kingdom is probably an example of such a country.) On the other hand, for countries that have to import much of their capital equipment, a rise in government outlays on infrastructure may well be expected to lead to a larger current account deficit at any given level of activity. (Australia is an example of such a country.)

It is, moreover, possible that the strengthening of the country's exchange rate consequent on the reduction in the government's claims for foreign exchange will have adverse effects on the profitability of domestic industry (unless that effect is offset by appropriate fiscal measures to ensure that this consequence does not follow). This may reduce output below capacity and have adverse consequences for the country in terms of both its level of employment and real output, and also of its net wealth.

Somewhat similar considerations apply to government measures that affect the level of private investment at any given level of activity. The most obvious of these are any forms of subsidies or tax concessions to private investment. A country that produces a high proportion of its requirements of capital goods is more likely to be able to give such a stimulus to investment without any comparable offsetting weakening of its current account, and is therefore likely to bring about a rise in its net wealth; whereas a country that imports a high proportion of investment goods can expect that the addition to the country's net wealth in the form of productive capital will be partly offset by the rise in net liabilities to the rest of the world resulting from the larger current account deficit. (It is of course possible that any such tax concessions or subsidies may be directed, inappropriately, to the less economic industries; it is only if the net effect is to raise the level of investment in economic ways that this sort of policy can be expected to increase national net wealth.)

The effects on the current account or national net wealth of different fiscal measures to stimulate investment are likely to vary greatly with the extent to which a country produces its own investment goods. This is likely to be a much more important consideration than whether the stimulus to investment is brought about by higher government infrastructure spending or by an increase in tax concessions to private investment.

There are likely also to be indirect effects on private investment resulting from changes in other types of taxation. In general, any measures that reduce the profitability of companies – either by increasing company/corporation tax or by higher taxes being imposed on employment (such as employers' national insurance contributions in Britain or social security taxes in continental Europe) are likely to make real investment less attractive to companies. (Increases in social security contributions by *employees* may also tend to lead to increases in money wage rates, and so business costs, and thus also reduce private investment indirectly.)

Any strengthening of the current account that may then result from the fall in investment and aggregate demand will be at least partly offset by the reduction in the country's stock of useful capital equipment; though it is likely that such measures as these will also reduce consumption spending – by the shareholders whose post-tax income is reduced by the rise in company tax or higher labour costs, or by those who are not now employed (because of the higher costs of employing them).

On balance, therefore, the downward effect on useful productive investment is, in this case, likely to be partially offset by the strengthening of the current account as consumption is held down, especially in countries where consumption has a high import content. For example, consumption goods have a high import content in Australia, and for Britain consumption spending on overseas holidays appears likely also to have a tendency to rise or fall especially sharply with changes in total consumption at the margin.

More generally, measures that reduce consumption will tend to improve the current account balance, and are less likely to have the adverse effects on net national wealth that result from any measures to strengthen the current account by reducing either public or private investment. For this reason they are likely to be less politically attractive than measures that curtail investment – much of the costs of which are in effect inflicted on posterity.

At the same time as trying to improve the net national wealth (or strengthen the current account balance) a government will normally be endeavouring to minimise any downward effect on output or employment, and any upward effect on inflation. For any given change in the budget balance, therefore, it should be trying to achieve that combination of measures that will have the desired effect on net wealth while keeping output and employment high and inflation reasonably low.

But it is not sufficient to consider only the combination of fiscal measures that will bring about the best balance of these macroeconomic objectives for a given state of the budget balance; for any given figure for the budget balance – or changes in it – if 'plucked out of the air' (so to speak) is unlikely to be that which brings about the best approximation to the achievement of the various macroeconomic objectives. It is more appropriate, therefore, to consider what changes in government outlays and receipts will best approximate those objectives, rather than whether the budget deficit/surplus should be somewhat higher or lower. For there will virtually always be combinations of changes in both government outlays and receipts, as well as in the balance between them, that will approximate more closely to the combination of results that is desired.

Against the social benefits to the future of bequeathing a lower level of public debt (and consequently of less need for taxation to service it) there should always be set the social benefits that can be achieved by somewhat larger government outlays (of appropriate types) or a somewhat lower level of taxation at the margin. By the same token, the social benefits of higher government outlays on worthwhile objectives, or lower taxes, needs to be set against the social costs (in the near and more distant future) of any rise in the level of public debt resulting from a consequently larger budget deficit. But the optimal result is unlikely to be achieved by simply picking a budget deficit target and merely considering alternative combinations of measures to achieve that balance with the most favourable or least unfavourable effect on the various macroeconomic objectives.

SOME EMPIRICAL EVIDENCE ABOUT THE EFFECTS OF DIFFERENT FISCAL MEASURES ON NET WEALTH

It may be seen from Table 6.1 that, over the five years after the change in policy, both these measures have, in each of the seven major OECD countries, an upward effect on the real current account deficit (or reduction in the surplus); and that for all these countries except Italy (for which the two effects are the same) a rise in government non-wage expenditure has a greater effect than income tax cuts in moving the current account balance in the direction of (greater) deficit.

One might expect that private consumption would have a higher import content than government non-wage expenditures, and therefore a greater effect on the current account for a given rise in expenditure. The explanation for the rise in government spending having a greater effect in increasing the current account deficit than do income tax cuts may lie at least partly in the fact that government spending has a greater upward effect on inflation and the price level than any rise in inflation that may result from income tax cuts of the same order. (See Tables 5.3 and 5.4.) One important reason for this may be that income tax cuts tend to restrain increases in money wage rates.

The direction of the effects on private investment of these two forms of fiscal stimulus vary considerably between countries, the effect on investment of increases in government non-wage expenditure and of income tax cuts in some countries being positive and in others negative. This should not be an unexpected result, for some forms of government outlay tend to increase the prospective profitability of private investment, whereas other forms of government expenditure may tend to 'crowd out' some forms of private investment; and income tax cuts financed by government borrowing may also 'crowd out' private investment, as well as stimulating it in other ways.

The two final lines give an estimate of the effect of these two measures on the current account plus private investment – or 'national net wealth'. It may be seen that government non-wage expenditures have for each country a less positive or greater negative effect on this combined total than do personal income tax cuts. If the government non-wage expenditures in question had been wholly on productive capital (human or material), in order to estimate the effect on total national net wealth a figure of the order expenditure on private net wealth shown in the table. It is quite likely that the ranking of government *investment* expenditures and of personal income tax cuts could for some or all countries be the reverse of those in the table for government consumption on the one hand and income tax cuts on the other – or that the gap between them would at any rate be much smaller.

Table 6.1: Simulated effects of government expenditure and income tax cuts on the real foreign balance and on private investment in seven major OECD countries
(Five-year totals as %ge of GDP for a rise in the government borrowing equal to 1% of GDP)
'A'=Government non-wage expenditure; 'B'=Cuts in personal income tax

	US	Japan	Germany	France	UK	Italy	Canada
Effects on –							
Real current account balance							
'A'	–0.42	–0.33	–0.57	–0.31	–0.37	–0.19	–0.32
'B'	–0.26	–0.25	–0.54	–0.27	–0.31	–0.19	–0.26
Private investment							
'A'	–0.06	–0.11	+0.09	+0.14	–0.08	+0.08	+0.09
'B'	–0.01	+0.03	+0.30	+0.28	–0.02	+0.20	+0.10
*'Net wealth'**							
'A'	–0.48	–0.44	–0.48	–0.17	–0.45	–0.11	–0.23
'B'	–0.27	–0.22	–0.24	+0.01	–0.33	+0.01	–0.16

* Effect on real current account balance plus effect on private investment.
Note: The simulated effects on private investment are %ge differences from baseline divided by the change in the government financial balance in terms of its deviation from baseline, as a %ge of GDP/GNP. The original data give percentage deviations of private investment from its own baseline value. These are converted to a percentage of baseline GDP by using the ratio of private fixed capital investment to GDP/GNP for 1985.
The simulations are those with fixed money supply and floating exchange rates.

Source: Data for government expenditure derived from Richardson (1987) and data for income tax cuts supplied by him.

The conclusion about the ranking of these measures in terms of their effect upon national net wealth should therefore be that government investment expenditures probably have the greatest upward (or smallest downward) effect, followed by personal income tax cuts, and then government non-wage consumption expenditures.

In any case, one should not draw conclusions from these simulations about the effects of *general* tax cuts, or increases in government outlays *in general*; for the effects on national net wealth of cuts in taxes other than income tax, and of government wage expenditures, could well be very different (as some of the other simulations used in this chapter suggest).

These figures may be used to illustrate how a movement of the budget in the direction of surplus will not necessarily strengthen the current account balance, still less increase net wealth, although it is often argued that the government should move the budget towards surplus with a view to strengthening the current account. Taking the UK as an example, and using the figures in Table 6.1, a rise in government non-wage expenditure equal to 1% of GDP accompanied by a somewhat greater rise in personal income tax (anything above 1% but less than 1.2%) would move the budget towards surplus, but still leave the current account balance weaker than before the change (the rise in government non-wage expenditure weakening the current account by 0.37% of GDP, and the rise in personal income tax strengthening it by something less than 0.37% of GDP).

If the effect on net wealth is the prime consideration for the UK, the figures for effects on net wealth would suggest that a rise in government non-wage (consumption) expenditure equal to 1% of GDP (reducing net wealth by 0.45% of GDP) accompanied by a somewhat greater rise in personal income tax (up to about 1.3% of GDP) would move the budget towards surplus (reduce the PSBR) but would also reduce net wealth, because the rise in taxation would increase net wealth by less than the rise in government spending would reduce it.

Similar illustrations could be given for each of the other countries, except that for Italy the two measures are estimated as having the same effect on the current account balance, so that any movement of the budget in the direction of surplus by the use of these two fiscal instruments would tend to strengthen the current account balance. But even for Italy there would be combinations of rises in government non-wage (consumption) expenditure coupled with (larger) increases in personal income tax that would move the budget towards surplus but still reduce net wealth on this measure.

Moreover, if the cuts in government outlays were on investment expenditures, there would be a range of cuts in government outlays accompanied by (somewhat smaller) cuts in personal income tax that would move the budget towards surplus (if the outlay side is defined to include investment expenditure), while reducing national net wealth.

The conclusions about the relative effects of these two instruments on the current account balance are confirmed by the results of simulations with various country models in the 1980s, summarised in Table 6.2. (These simulations do not give the effects on private investment, with the addition of which one could have estimated the effects on national net wealth.)

Table 6.2: Simulated effects on current account balance of various OECD countries of increases in government expenditure and cuts in personal income tax
(Change in current account balance as %ge of GDP/GNP for an average 1% stimulus to real GDP/GNP over Years 1, 2, 3 & 7, with the change in the current account balance over that period for an initial fiscal change equal to 1% of GDP in parentheses)

	US	Japan	France	UK	Canada 1	Canada 2
Real government	−4.39	−0.56	−4.79	−1.41	−5.60	−1.76
expenditure	(−3.91)	(−1.32)	(−8.14)	(−1.15)	(−3.08)	(−3.06)
Personal income	−3.42	−0.39	−8.13	−1.98	−6.14	−3.04
tax cuts	(−2.82)	(−0.56)	(−4.09)	(−1.11)	(−3.49)	(−3.03)

Source: Derived from Chan-Lee and Kato (1984).

In all these simulations, except that with one of the models for Canada, personal income tax cuts have a smaller upward effect than does government expenditure on the current account deficit for an initial stimulus equal to 1% of GDP. But in relation to the average stimulus to real GDP over the five years, government expenditure has the larger effect on the current account only for the US and Japan. If, therefore, a government wishes to provide a stimulus with minimal adverse effect on the current account for a given initial rise in the budget deficit over the period, it will do better to cut personal income tax than raise government non-wage outlays. But if its aim is to provide a given stimulus to real GDP with as little effect as possible in increasing the current account deficit in the medium term, it would, on these figures, prefer to increase government spending, except in the US and Japan.

EVIDENCE FOR THE EEC IN THE MID-1980s

It may be seen from the simulation drawn upon in Table 6.3 that, for the EEC in the mid-1980s, a cut in employers' social security contributions had a large upward effect on private investment, far in excess of its estimated effect in moving the current account towards deficit, so that this policy measure, taken alone, could be expected to have an upward effect on national net wealth (as indicated by the sum of its effects on private investment and its effect on the current account). It would, however, move the current account towards deficit to a greater extent than a cut in household income tax. Cuts in household indirect taxation had a slightly greater effect in increasing the current account deficit than cuts in household direct taxation, but a greater upward

Table 6.3: Simulated effects of various fiscal measures on private investment, the current account balance and net wealth in the EEC
(Five-year total as %ge of GDP for a rise in budget deficit equal to 1% of GDP)

	Current account (1)	Investment (2)	'Net wealth' (3) =(1)+(2)
Cut in employers' social security contributions	−0.40	+0.81	+0.41
Cut in household direct tax	−0.38	+0.17	−0.21
Cut in household indirect tax	−0.41	+0.37	−0.04
Public investment*	−1.77	+1.23	−0.54
Public consumption	−1.77	+0.23	−1.54

Note: The figures for private investment are given in the source as percentages of baseline private investment. In column (3) they have here been converted to the approximate equivalent as a %ge of GDP by the using the ratio of Gross Private Fixed Capital Formation to GDP in 1986 from OECD *Historical Statistics*.
*Estimated on the assumption that the effects on private investment and on the current account balance are the same as for public consumption. The public investment equal to 1% of GDP is therefore added to the total for net wealth.

Source: Derived from Dramais (1986).

effect on private investment, so that the effect of cuts in household indirect taxation on national net wealth was very small (and, bearing in mind the margins of error in such simulations, it would perhaps be reasonable to say that it would be slightly positive or slightly negative). Public consumption had a slightly greater positive effect on private investment than a cut in household direct taxation, but a larger unfavourable effect on the current account balance (in this latter respect thus confirming the result we found from Tables 6.1 and 6.2).

In the model with which these simulations are made, public consumption is not distinguished from public investment. The estimate given in the table for effects of public investment is therefore based on the assumption that its effects on the current account and on private investment are the same as those of government consumption. A rise in public investment might either increase or reduce private investment to a greater extent than would public consumption; but if its effects on these were (on balance) the same as for public consumption, one could then add the effect of a rise in public investment equal to 1% of GDP, increasing the figure for the change in national net wealth in column

(3) to 1.23% of GDP instead of the 0.23% for public consumption. This would suggest that a rise in government investment outlays would, on these figures, still have a greater downward effect on net wealth than would any of the tax measures simulated, for a given effect on the budget balance (though, of course, a much smaller downward effect than if the outlays consisted of public consumption).

It should be borne in mind, however, that this simulation is for a large (and to that extent relatively 'closed') economy, and that the results could well be very different for individual countries. It is quite possible that for an individual country the private expenditures stimulated by the tax cuts would have a much higher import content than government outlays.

The figures in Table 6.3 thus illustrate that:

1   A reduction in government borrowing (reduction in the budget deficit) will not necessarily strengthen the current account. A shift from household direct taxation to household indirect taxation (for a given budget balance) would tend to strengthen the current account (the cut in household direct taxation increasing the current account deficit by less than it would be reduced by a rise in indirect taxation of the same size). There would therefore be some combinations of the two (ones in which income taxation rose slightly more than indirect taxes were cut) that would increase the current account deficit while reducing the budget deficit (the cut in indirect taxation increasing the current account deficit by more than it was reduced by the rise in income tax). Moreover, a rise in taxation equal to 1% of GDP will strengthen the current account by less than it will be weakened by a rise in government outlays equal to just under 1% of GDP. The budget deficit will then *fall* (tax receipts rising by more than the rise in government outlays), but the current account deficit would *increase*.

2   Some ways of reducing the budget deficit will *reduce* net wealth. Obviously a rise in employers' social security contributions would do so. On these figures, a shift from direct to indirect household taxation could also be found that would reduce net wealth while also reducing the budget deficit – as the rise in national net wealth resulting from a rise in household indirect taxation would be less than the downward effect on net wealth of a somewhat smaller cut in direct taxation. (The budget deficit falls, as total tax proceeds rise; but net wealth falls.)

Furthermore, as public (consumption) outlays reduce national wealth by more than the equivalent household tax cuts, a rise in government outlays of 1% of GDP will reduce the stock of national wealth by more than it will be increased by a slightly greater rise in taxes. The budget would move towards surplus (government outlays rising by less than revenue), but national wealth would fall.

Similarly, on the same assumptions, a cut in government consumption equal to 1% of GDP that was accompanied by a cut in taxes equal to something more than 1% of GDP (more than twice as much for household direct tax as for government consumption) would increase the budget deficit (revenue falling by more than outlays), but could also increase national net wealth, for the upward effect on net wealth of the cut in government consumption would exceed the downward effect on net wealth of the tax cut equal to something over 1% of GDP. The consequent move towards *deficit* in the budget (revenue falling by more than outlays) would thus be accompanied by an *increase* in national net wealth.

If, therefore, a government wishes to reduce the budget deficit, it will do well to consider also whether it wants to strengthen the current account or increase national net wealth (or both); and choose the combinations of fiscal measures accordingly, as they will be different according to which of those other objectives it considers the more important. In any case, the so-called 'twin-deficits' theory – that a reduction in the budget deficit tends to strengthen the current account (in some formulations, even to the same extent) – is seen to be by no means generally true.

EVIDENCE FOR THE UNITED STATES

Results from simulations by McKibbin and Bagnoli (1993) for the US are shown in Table 6.4.

The figures in Table 6.4 are only very approximate, as many of them are read off graphs. (There is no obvious reason to believe that the ranking of these instruments in terms of their effects on the current account would be substantially different from their ranking in terms of their effects on the trade balance – though one would prefer to know the effects on the total current account as a more adequate indicator of an important aspect of their effects on national net wealth.) The variations as between the effects of the various measures on private investment and the trade balance (for a given rise in the budget deficit) are, however, clear enough to enable one to draw certain broad conclusions.

Investment tax credits, a permanent labour tax credit and cuts in corporation tax have favourable effects on private investment, though they also move the trade balance towards deficit to a greater extent than most of the others. But the stimulus to private investment from any of the top four measures is so great as to move this indicator of national net wealth (private investment less any rise in the trade deficit) in a positive direction. Investment tax credits clearly stimulate private investment more than the other measures. Cuts in indirect taxation also have an upward effect on private investment, but they have an upward effect on the trade deficit sufficient to make their effect on the combined total negative.

Table 6.4: Simulated effects of various fiscal measures on private investment and the trade balance of the US

(%ge of GDP for rise in budget deficit equal to 1% of GDP, five-year totals)

	Private investment (1)	Trade balance (2)	'Net wealth' = (1)+(2)
Investment tax credit			
– permanent	+4.96	–1.86	+3.10
– temporary	+3.24	–1.07	+2.17
Corporation tax cut	+0.91	–0.45	+0.46
Labour tax credit			
– permanent	+0.39	–0.35	+0.04
– temporary	+0.15	–0.22	–0.07
Government non-investment spending*	0.16	–0.28	–0.11
	(+0.24)	(–0.29)	(–0.05)
Cut in indirect taxation	+0.56	–0.70	–0.14
Lump-sum transfers to households	+0.24	–0.41	–0.17
Income tax cut	–0.06	–0.33	–0.26
Government infrastructure investment			
– cut-off	–0.12	–0.17	–0.29
	(+0.88)		(+0.71)
– gradual	–0.73	–0.18	–0.91
	(+0.27)		(+0.09)

Figures in parentheses are for effect on net wealth including government capital.
* See note to Table 3.7.

The indirect taxation simulation in the original source is for the introduction of a VAT. The signs have therefore been reversed in the above table.

Source: Derived from graphical data in McKibbin, and Bagnoli (1993) and underlying data supplied by them.

A cut in income tax (of the type being simulated – which is one that mainly benefits higher income groups) has the largest unfavourable effect on net wealth (on this measure) of the various tax cuts and tax credits simulated, its small negative effect on private investment and its upward effect on the trade deficit giving it the largest negative effect on the combined total (including public capital).

Government infrastructure investment has a small downward effect on private investment, to which must be added its positive effect on public capital investment, and a smaller upward effect on the trade deficit than the other measures simulated.

Government non-investment expenditure and temporary labour tax credits have a positive effect on private investment, but a large enough effect in the direction of increasing the trade deficit for their effect on the combined total to be slightly negative.

Government infrastructure investment has by far the most unfavourable effect on private investment, but an upward effect on total (including government) investment, ranking below only an investment tax credit in its effects on total net wealth on this broader measure.

The figures in parentheses for government infrastructure investment are to take account also of the direct effects on capital formation of the government infrastructure investment equal to 1% of GDP. When this adjustment is made, government infrastructure investment is the only one of the measures of government outlay simulated here having an upward effect on total investment, and also on net wealth, as well as having a smaller upward effect on the current account deficit than any of the other measures simulated.

The much greater positive effect on total net wealth of government infrastructure investment than that of other forms of government spending makes it especially important not to choose to reduce the budget deficit by cutting government infrastructure investment if the aim is to avoid reductions in total national net wealth – despite its adverse effect on private investment and private net wealth. There are clearly a number of measures of fiscal tightening that would, on this measure, *reduce* private net wealth (the top four in the table) whereas a tightening of any of the other measures would increase it.

It may thus be seen that the ranking of these measures in terms of their effects on the trade balance is very different from their effect on the combined total. It is therefore likely that if the choice of measures were directed towards reducing the budget deficit in the manner most likely to reduce the trade deficit, the choice would be one that would adversely affect national wealth on this measure. For example, if any of the top four measures in this table were used to reduce the budget deficit, although that would reduce the trade deficit it would also reduce net wealth on this measure.

If one aim is to reduce the current account deficit, so far as the effects on the trade balance may be taken as indicative of the relative effects on the current account balance, it may be seen that a reduction in the budget deficit will not necessarily strengthen the current account balance. For example, an increase in corporation tax or indirect taxation would have a relatively large effect in strengthening the current account; whereas a cut in government infrastructure investment (or non-investment expenditure), or a rise of the same order in income tax, could be expected to have a much smaller effect in strengthening the current account. There will thus be many combinations of *cuts* in government infrastructure investment or non-investment expenditure, coupled with *rather smaller cuts* in corporation tax or indirect taxation that would reduce the budget deficit but *increase* the current account deficit. For those tax cuts would have a large effect in increasing the current account deficit, whereas the cuts in government spending would do relatively little to strengthen it.

Moreover, there would be many combinations of measures to reduce the budget deficit that would *reduce* net wealth. This would be true of many combinations of tightening of measures near the top of the table in combination with a somewhat lesser tightening of measures nearer to the bottom of the table. For a move to reduce the budget deficit by such a combination of measures would do more to reduce (or less to increase) national wealth, through the tightening of measures near the top of the table, than any increases in it resulting from the tightening of measures nearer the bottom of the table.

EVIDENCE FOR SOME SMALLER COUNTRIES

Evidence for Belgium

Table 6.5 shows for Belgium the widely divergent effects upon both gross capital formation and net exports of the six fiscal measures simulated. For state investment, the upward effects upon capital formation, both private and public, greatly outweigh the extent of its downward effect on net exports; in other words, if a government aiming to reduce a current account deficit did so by reducing state investment it would have a seriously adverse effect on both capital formation and net wealth.

Although state investment clearly has the greatest effect in reducing net exports (for a given effect on the budget balance), it is followed fairly closely by social security transfers to households, with all the other measures simulated having only about half as great a downward effect on net exports.

Table 6.5: Simulated effects of various fiscal measures on gross capital formation and net exports as a %ge of GDP for Belgium
(Five-year average for change in public sector deficit equal to 1% of GDP)

	Gross capital formation*	Net exports	Net wealth
Rise in state investment	1.76	−1.12	0.64
Cut in personal income tax	0.31	−0.68	−0.37
Cut in employers' social security contributions	0.15	−0.53	−0.38
Cut in VAT on private consumption products	−0.08	−0.61	−0.53
Rise in public employment	−0.25	−0.69	−0.94
Rise in social security payments to households	−0.39	−0.95	−1.34

*Effect on capital formation (public plus private) converted to a %ge of GDP by the ratio of gross fixed capital formation to GDP in 1986.

In the original the policy changes were in the opposite direction to those shown here: the signs have therefore been reversed in the table above.

Source: Bogaert et al. (1990).

The importance of distinguishing between public sector investment and public sector employment is well illustrated in this table – public employment having a large downward effect on capital formation, in contrast to the upward effect of state investment, leading to a rise in national net wealth on this measure. In the light of this, the downward effect of public sector investment on net exports is relatively insignificant if the aim is to keep up the level of national net wealth.

Of the three tax cuts simulated, cuts in personal income tax and in employers' social security contributions have an upward effect on capital formation, whereas cuts in VAT on household products have a downward effect on capital formation relative to GDP, having an especially large upward effect on private consumption. Income tax cuts have only a slightly greater downward effect on net exports than do cuts in employers' social security contributions, though appreciably more than a cut in VAT. But income tax cuts stimulate capital formation to a greater extent than any of the other measures apart from public investment. (This is consistent with the results for five of the seven countries shown in Table 6.1, where personal income tax cuts had a positive effect on private investment.)

Both government expenditure on employment and social security transfers to households had a greater effect in the direction of reducing net exports (and thus, presumably, increasing the current account deficit), and also, on this evidence, in reducing net wealth, than did either of the tax cuts simulated.

EVIDENCE RELATING TO THE CURRENT ACCOUNT BALANCE ALONE

The results reported in earlier sections of this chapter, for cases where effects on both private investment and the current account (or at least the trade balance) have been simulated for various fiscal changes, make it possible to make an estimate of the ranking of some fiscal measures in terms of their effect on net national wealth (effects on investment, or at least on private investment, plus or minus any effect on the current account balance). The figures shown in earlier tables of this chapter show that there is not necessarily a close connection between the ranking in terms of the effects on investment, on the one hand, and the effects on the current account, on the other; though there appears to be some tendency for the measures that have the greatest upward effect on investment to have the greatest effect in increasing a current account deficit (or reducing any surplus); and the ranking in terms of the combined effect on these two magnitudes together is generally different again. The minimal conclusion can, however, be drawn that, as different fiscal measures have different effects on investment, the current account and net wealth for a given effect on public sector borrowing, it is not helpful to think of a reduction of public sector borrowing as a means of improving the current account, as there will be combinations of fiscal measures that will reduce government borrowing, while worsening the current account; and even those combinations that strengthen the current account may reduce private investment, or net wealth or both.

But, bearing in mind these problems with using the effects on the current account alone as a guide to policy, it may be of use to summarise some of the estimates for the effects of fiscal measures on the current account in some countries, where the simulations in question do not also provide simulations of the effects on private investment. For governments do in fact consider the effects of their policies on the current account of the balance of payments, and provided that this is complemented by assessments of the other aspects of the effects on fiscal measures on net national wealth, this may be of some use as a guide to policy.

Knoester and Kolodziejac (1994) have produced results for the effects on the current account of public spending and cuts in direct taxation for Europe (the EEC as at the mid-1980s), Japan and the US (though effects on private investment are not shown). These are given in Table 6.6.

Table 6.6 shows that, for Japan and the EEC over the five years, government expenditure tended to increase the current account deficit (or, of course, reduce any surplus) by more than cuts in direct taxation. These results are consistent with those shown in Table 6.1, in which the simulations showed that for all but one of the major European (and other) countries government non-wage expenditure moved the current account balance in the direction of deficit by more than did cuts in personal income tax. But the simulation reported in Table 6.6 presumably covers a broader range of government spending than that simulated in Table 6.1.

Table 6.6: Simulated effects of government expenditure and income tax cuts
upon the real foreign balance of the EEC, Japan and the US
(Total of Years 1 to 5 as % of GDP for fall of 1% of GDP in
the government financial balance)

	EEC	Japan	US
Public spending	−0.33	−0.22	−0.11
Direct tax cuts	−0.12	−0.10	−0.28

Source: Derived from Knoester and Kolodziejac (1994).

For the US (as was also true of the evidence in Table 6.4), direct tax cuts had a greater effect than government spending in the direction of weakening the current account balance. By contrast, in Table 6.1, government *non-wage* expenditure in the US had a bigger effect on the current account balance than cuts in personal income tax. This may mean that, for the US, government expenditure on wages has a greater effect in weakening the current account than government non-wage expenditures. (Comparisons with Table 6.4 for the US are not readily made, as the categorisation of government outlays used, as well as the sort of direct tax cuts simulated, are very different between the two tables.)

Furthermore, these results for the US cannot be directly compared with those in Table 6.1 because the results in Table 6.6 are available only for years 1 and 5, whereas those used in Table 6.1 are for the five-year totals.

An earlier simulation by Knoester (1988) is reported in Table 6.7.

It may be seen from this table that public spending has a larger apparent effect on the current account balance in year 1 than does a cut in direct taxation for both Europe and the US, but that the reverse is true for Japan. In the fifth year after the change, however, the cuts in direct taxation have the greater effect of the two for Europe, whereas public spending has the greater effect for Japan. Taken together with earlier tables, this suggests that the relative size of the effect on the current account of these two fiscal measures may be expected to vary with the period under consideration, and also from one country to another.

Table 6.7: Simulated effects of public spending and direct tax cuts on current account balance for Europe, Japan and the US
(As %ge of GDP for a rise in the budget deficit equal to 1% of GDP)

	Europe		US		Japan	
	Year 1	Year 5	Year 1	Year 5	Year 1	Year 5
Public spending	−0.3	-0.5	−0.3	−0.6	−0.1	−0.7
Cuts in direct taxation	−0.1	−0.6	−0.1	−0.5	−0.2	−0.3

In each case the figures represent the ratio of the change in the current account balance as a percentage of GDP to the change in the budget deficit as a percentage of GDP.

Source: Derived from Knoester (1988).

EVIDENCE FOR THE CURRENT ACCOUNT BALANCE IN THE UK

The simulations by the Macroeconomic Modelling Bureau of the University of Warwick with various UK models do not give figures for the effects of various fiscal measures on private investment. They do, however, give figures for effects on the current account balance. (See Table 6.8.)

For a given change in the PSBR, the effects on the current account balance of the three tax cuts simulated vary greatly between models. In three models a cut in income tax increases the current account deficit by less than the two other types of tax cut. But each type of tax cut has the least effect on the current account in at least one model, and the greatest effect of the three in at least one other. No firm conclusion, therefore, can be drawn from this evidence about the relative effects on the current account balance of each of these types of tax cut for a given change in the PSBR. On balance, however, the evidence implies that a cut in personal income tax probably had less effect in increasing the current account deficit for a given change in the PSBR than either of the other two types of tax cut. (We shall find in Chapter 8 a different result for the effects on the current account *for a given stimulus given to real GDP*.)

The principal conclusion to be derived from Table 6.8, showing the simulated effects on the current account balance for Britain, is that government expenditure for that country probably had a greater upward effect on the current account deficit for a given rise in the PSBR than did income tax cuts (a result clearly consistent with that for the UK in Table 6.1), though the other two tax cuts may have had as great an effect. As we shall see in Chapter 8, however, government spending had the smallest effect on the current account balance *in relation to the stimulus it gave to real GDP*.

Table 6.8: Simulated effects on current account of various fiscal measures in the UK
(Five-year total effect on current account balance in billion pounds sterling for 1% rise in PSBR, total of first five years)

	LBS	NIESR	HMT	BE**	OEF	STR	Average
Government expenditure*	−1.26	−2.00	−0.62	−2.20	−1.12	−0.76	−1.33
Personal income tax cuts	−0.32	−1.50	−0.54	−0.72	−0.71	−2.01	−0.97
Cut in VAT	−0.08	−1.52	−0.76	−1.56	−2.01	−1.13	−1.18
Cut in employers' national insurance contributions	−0.44	−1.25	−0.67	−1.92	−0.92	−1.00	−1.03

*Simulation with fixed nominal interest rates.
**Four years only for BE model.
For key to models, see Table 3.8.

Source: Derived from Church et al. (1993).

Table 6.9 shows that for all the five countries (with the exception of one of the two models for Canada) for which these simulations with individual country models are available, with a non-accommodating monetary policy a cut in personal income tax has a smaller effect in increasing the current account deficit (or reducing any surplus) than a rise in government non-wage expenditures equal to 1% of GDP (a result consistent with Table 6.1).

These simulations do not give figures for the effect on the budget deficit in each year of the simulations, so that the results are not exactly comparable with those of most of the other simulations. They do, however, show the simulated effect on the current account balance of alternative fiscal stimuli equal to 1% of GDP in the year in which the change of policy takes place. We saw in Table 3.4, however, that in every case but one (one of the two models for Canada), government outlays had a greater effect on real GDP than did income tax cuts; and we saw in Table 5.4 that (again with the exception of one of the two models for Canada) government outlays had a greater upward effect on prices than did income tax cuts. This higher level of real and nominal GDP resulting from government spending than that from personal income tax cuts (for the same rise in the budget deficit in the initial year) means that tax revenue would be higher, and so the budget deficit smaller, in subsequent years for a given rise in government (non-wage) spending than with one provided by a cut in income tax having the same effect on the budget deficit in the initial year.

Table 6.9: Simulated effects of certain forms of fiscal stimulus on current account balance of certain OECD countries, with non-accommodating monetary policy (Averages of Years 1, 2, 3 & 7 of %ge deviations from baseline for a change in government financial balance equal to 1% of GDP in first year)

	Government non-wage expenditure	Personal income tax cuts
US	−3.91	−2.82
Japan	−1.32	−0.55
France	−8.14	−4.09
UK	−1.15	−1.11
Canada 1	−3.08	−3.43
Canada 2	−3.06	−3.03

The simulations used are those with floating exchange rates.
Note: In the original, the simulations are for *increases* in personal income tax and *reductions* in government non-wage expenditure. The signs have therefore been reversed in the above table. The models used are those from individual countries, two different models being used for Canada.

Source: Derived from Chan-Lee and Kato (1984).

The relative effect of government spending on the current account (as also its effects on real output or prices) for a given effect on the budget deficit over the whole period of years would thus be considerably greater, relative to that of personal income tax cuts, than the comparison shown in Table 6.9 would suggest (as that reflects their relative effect only in terms of the change in the budget deficit in the year the change is made).

Such figures as these illustrate the folly of governments thinking that by increasing the budget surplus (or reducing the deficit) – especially by reducing the budget deficit in a single year – they can necessarily reduce the current account deficit in the balance of payments.

Take, for example, some figures based on the relative order of magnitude of the ones for the US in Table 6.9, showing the effects of each of these measures upon the current account. If a given rise in government spending weakens the balance of payments by an amount equal to 4% of GDP, whereas a rise in personal income tax of the same size strengthens it by an amount equal to only 3% of GDP, a balanced budget increase using these two fiscal measures would, on balance, increase the current account deficit by an amount equal to 1% of GDP. This also means that if income tax were reduced by rather more than government spending (up to a third more than the cut in government spending), the budget would move in the direction of deficit, but the current account would be strengthened. Similarly, if the budget were moved in the direction of surplus, by increasing income tax by somewhat more than a given rise in government spending (up to one and a third times as much as the rise in government spending), the budget would move in the direction of surplus (revenue rising more than outlays), but the current account would move further in the direction of deficit (or reduced surplus).

EVIDENCE FROM NORDIC COUNTRIES

Table 6.10 drawing upon simulations with the various models for the Nordic countries shows a variety of rankings of the three fiscal instruments simulated in terms of their effects on the current account balance. In one model, government employment expenditure has the smallest upward effect on the current account deficit, whereas in all the other models it has the largest effect (in one case the equal largest). Of the two types of tax cuts simulated, in all models except one a cut in VAT increases the current account deficit by less than a cut in local income tax for a given effect on the budget balance. It is, however, possible to rank fiscal instruments in terms of their effects on net wealth by looking at only their effects on the current account balance.

*Table 6.10: Simulated effects of certain fiscal measures on
the current account balance of four Nordic countries*
(%ge of GDP for a 1% of GDP rise in budget deficit)

Model:	ADAM	MODAG	KOSMOS	KESSU	BOF4
Rise in government employment expenditure	−0.90	−0.87	−0.68	−0.69	−0.82
Cut in local income tax	−2.06	−0.38	−0.68	−0.36	−0.41
Cut in VAT	−2.05	−0.25	−0.49	−0.43	−0.15

For key to models see Table 3.12.

Source: Derived from Wallis and Whitley (1991).

CONCLUSIONS

The evidence from those simulations for which we have found evidence relating to the effects of various fiscal measures on both the current account (or in some cases the trade balance) and the level of investment (either private or public both) may be summarised as follows. (See Table 6.11.)

The most important items to note in this list are that public infrastructure investment ranks at or near the top (as having the greatest upward or least downward effect on national net wealth), whereas other forms of public outlay rank near the bottom of that ranking. Valid generalisations about government spending in aggregate terms are thus not possible.

As to the effects on private investment, government non-wage expenditure has a more unfavourable (or less favourable) effect in all the countries than income tax cuts, which increase private investment in each country.

Putting these two effects together (as a measure of the change in the country's net wealth), it may be seen that government non-wage expenditure in each case reduces net wealth, while personal income tax cuts reduce it by less, or even increase it.

Table 6.11: Ranking order of effects of various fiscal measures on net wealth for a given change in the budget balance
(Expansionary measures with greatest upward or least downward effect on net wealth at or near the top)

1	Government investment expenditure
2	Investment tax credit
3	Cut in employers' social security or national insurance contributions
4	Cut in company or corporation tax
5	Labour tax credit
6	Personal income tax cut
7	Indirect tax cuts
8	Government non-wage expenditures
9	Government employment expenditures
10	Government consumption
11	Social security transfers

7 The Relevance of the Setting of Monetary Policy and Exchange Rate Policy

The effects on the various macroeconomic objectives of any given change in a government outlay or revenue item depend in part on the setting of monetary policy and the exchange rate policy that accompanies the change in the fiscal measures.

Considering first the role of monetary policy, at one extreme a rise in outlay or a cut in revenue that is financed wholly by the creation of additional money – on a scale that prevents any rise in nominal interest rates – is likely to lead to a greater upward pressure on capacity and on prices (or a smaller reduction in them) than the same change in a fiscal item when monetary policy is tighter. This is termed an 'accommodating' monetary policy.

If, on the other hand, the setting of monetary policy is such that interest rates are permitted to rise under the impetus of the fiscal expansion (especially if they do so sufficiently for the whole of the rise in government outlays or cut in taxes to be financed by additional sales of government bonds), the increase in interest rates will offset at least part of the expansionary effect of the tax cut or the rise in government outlays. This is termed a 'non-accommodating' monetary policy. In this case, the net upward effect on employment or output will therefore normally be less than if the setting of monetary policy had been easier, and the additional government borrowing may even 'crowd out' so much private expenditure that there is no rise in output or employment. It is conceivable that there could even be a net reduction in real output or employment if private expenditure is very sensitive to increases in interest rates, especially if the forms of government outlay that are increased, or the taxes that are cut, are ones that do not have much upward effect on private spending.

But this leaves open the question whether the setting of monetary policy has any bearing on the *relative* effects upon output or employment of different forms of government outlays or taxes. If a rise in government outlays of a million currency units tends to be more inflationary than a tax cut of the same amount, then nominal interest rates will tend to rise more under this more inflationary alternative. It seems preferable to define an 'accommodating' monetary policy as one that holds real (rather than nominal) interest rates constant in the face of a change in fiscal policy.

Of course, monetary policy may be set somewhere between the two extremes considered above – that is to say, where real interest rates are permitted to rise to some extent, but not as much as if monetary policy was completely 'non-accommodating' (which may be roughly equivalent to some, but not all, of the rise in government outlays or reduction in revenue being financed by additional government borrowing from the public). One would then expect any given rise in an outlay or fall in a revenue item to have a smaller upward effect on output and employment than it would have done if the fiscal change in question has been wholly accommodated by monetary measures to hold real interest rates down; but greater than it would have been if it had been wholly financed by borrowing from the public.

But, from the present point of view, the important consideration is whether the method of financing changes the relative advantages of using a rise in a particular form of government outlay or a fall in a particular source of government revenue (having the same effect on the budget balance) in terms of their impact on the various macroeconomic objectives. It is not easy to think of any a priori reason why the ranking of different fiscal instruments should be changed by the method of financing chosen; but it would certainly be surprising if the relative effect of each of them on inflation (for example) for a given stimulus to output or employment, or for a given effect on the budget deficit, were exactly the same under all possible methods of financing.

Most of the simulations on which we have drawn in earlier chapters do not consider alternative settings of monetary policy in simulations of more than one instrument of policy. There are, however, three sets of simulations that do so, all emanating from the OECD (one in the mid-1980s, and giving the alternatives of fixed interest rates or a fixed quantity of money); the two others from the 1990s (from OECD *Working Papers* No. 144 and 148 of 1994) which give parallel simulations of two fiscal instruments, one of them giving results for both instruments with monetary policy set to hold real interest rates constant, and the other using the assumption that interest rates are allowed to change in the face of the fiscal measures (that is, monetary policy is 'non-accommodating').

The top half of Table 7.1 shows the effect on real output of these two fiscal measures over five years, if monetary policy is 'accommodating' – that is, holding real interest rates constant (in effect, increasing purchases of government bonds by the central bank to negate the upward effects on real interest rates of the fiscal expansion, and so eliminate the 'crowding out' effect that would otherwise result from the increase in interest rates). On this assumption about monetary policy, the effect of government non-wage expenditure is (in this simulation) just over half as great as the effect of a direct tax rise having the same effect on the budget balance.

Table 7.1: Simulated effects of two fiscal measures on the rate of increase of real GDP in the OECD, with different settings of monetary policy
(%ge effect over five years for a change in government net lending over the period equal to 1% of GDP, with effect in Year 5 in parentheses)

With unchanged real interest rates:	
Rise in government non-wage expenditure	0.56 (0.22)
Cut in direct taxation	0.98 (0.40)
With real interest rates allowed to	
rise with the fiscal expansion:	
Rise in government non-wage expenditure	0.13 (0.18)
Cut in direct taxation	0.44 (0.31)

Note: The simulations in the original source are those with slower (or 'low') growth. They were for cuts in government outlays and tax increases. The signs have therefore been reversed in the above table.

Source: Derived from Richardson et al. (1994).

But if the setting of monetary policy is such as to allow interest rates to rise in response to the fiscal expansion, the rate of growth of real GDP over the period is considerably less than with an accommodating monetary policy; and a tax cut increases output by less than half as much as if real interest rates had been prevented from rising by an easing of monetary policy.

With unchanged real interest rates, a rise in government non-wage outlays has just over half as great an effect on real GDP as that resulting from a cut in tax having the same effect on the budget balance over the whole period or in the fifth year after the change. But if the setting of monetary policy is such that real interest rates are allowed to rise with a fiscal expansion, a rise in government non-wage expenditure increases real output by only about a third of the effect of a cut in direct taxation over the full five years, though by over half as much as a tax cut by the end of the fifth year after the change. This change of assumption about monetary policy thus does not change the ranking of these two fiscal measures.

This also means that, when a budget deficit is being cut, the comparative advantage in minimising the downward effect on output of cutting government non-wage outlays (rather than increasing this particular package of direct taxation) is thus greater if real interest rates are allowed to rise than if they are held constant.

Similarly, the effect on inflation of each of the two fiscal instruments tested varies according to the setting of monetary policy. If real interest rates are held constant (that is, prevented by monetary policy from rising in response to the fiscal expansion) a rise in government outlays increases inflation over the period by more than twice as much as does a rise in taxation having the same effect on the budget balance. By contrast, if the real rate of interest is allowed to rise in response to the fiscal expansion, the reduction in inflation when government non-wage expenditure is increased is only about a fifth of that brought about by a cut in taxation of the same size. By the fifth year after the change, however, if interest rates are allowed to increase, the rise in government non-wage expenditures has a greater downward effect on the rate of inflation than does the cut in direct taxation.

If, of the other hand, monetary policy is 'non-accommodating' (in the sense that interest rates are allowed to rise in the face of the fiscal expansion), a rise in government non-wage expenditure will not reduce inflation over the five years as much as will cuts in this package of direct taxation; and government non-wage expenditure will lead to a rise in inflation by the fifth year, despite the downward impact on inflation of the rise in interest rates.

Table 7.2: Simulated effects of two fiscal measures on inflation in the OECD over five years, with different settings of monetary policy
(%ge effect for 1% of GDP rise in government borrowing, with effect in Year 5 in parentheses)

With unchanged real interest rates:	
Rise in government non-wage expenditures	+0.89 (+0.44)
Cut in direct taxation	+0.36 (+0.27)
With higher real interest rates:	
Rise in government non-wage expenditures	–0.09 (+0.09)
Cut in direct taxation	–0.49 (–0.07)

Notes and source: as for Table 7.1.

This also means that (as may be seen by reversing the signs in Table 7.2) if increases in these forms of direct taxation are used to reduce the budget deficit, with monetary policy being set so as to allow interest rates to fall in the face of the fiscal contraction, direct tax increases would increase inflation more than would cuts in government non-wage expenditure; and that by the fifth year a cut in government non-wage expenditures (but not a rise in direct taxation) could be expected to reduce inflation.

It may thus be seen that the ranking of these two instruments over five years is the same whether or not one assumes that monetary policy is accommodating (though not the ranking or the direction of their respective effects by the fifth year).

EVIDENCE FOR THE SEVEN MAJOR OECD COUNTRIES

We saw in Table 3.3 that, *with a fixed money supply*, over a five-year period changes in personal income tax had a greater effect on real GDP than did changes in government non-wage expenditures for a given effect on the government's financial balance over that period in five of the seven countries, but that the reverse was true for the US and Canada.

It may be seen from Table 7.3, however, that if *interest rates* are held constant, for all these countries except Italy, government non-wage expenditure increases real GDP by *more* than personal income tax cuts for a given effect on the budget balance (whether one considers the effect on the budget balance over the whole five years or only that in the first year).

Table 7.3: Simulated effects on real GDP of two fiscal instruments in the seven major OECD countries, with interest rates held constant by monetary policy and floating exchange rates
(Average change in real GDP over five years as % of baseline, for a change over that period in the government's financial balance equal to 1% of GDP; with change in relation to rise in budget deficit equal to 1% of GDP in first year in parentheses)

	Rise in government non-wage expenditure	Cut in personal income tax
US	2.60 (9.29)	2.29 (7.11)
Japan	2.47 (9.89)	2.05 (8.44)
Germany	2.57 (7.37)	2.04 (6.33)
France	0.85 (5.00)	0.80 (4.27)
UK	1.23 (5.89)	1.07 (5.00)
Italy	0.56 (3.69)	0.64 (3.82)
Canada	1.40 (5.78)	0.82 (4.00)

Source: Figures for effects of government expenditures derived from Richardson (1987); figures for effects of personal income tax cuts kindly supplied by that author on the basis of analogous simulations completed at the same time as those for government expenditures. The simulations used are those assuming fixed interest rates and floating exchange rates.

It therefore appears that the assumption made about monetary policy may – at least on this definition, of the effects on monetary policy on the quantity of money – change the ranking of these two instruments in terms of their effects on *real GDP*.

We saw in Table 4.3 (with the *money supply* held constant) that in five of the countries the effect of the non-wage government outlays on *employment* was greater than that of cuts in personal income tax, but that the reverse was true for Italy, while for Japan neither measure appears to have had a significant effect on *unemployment*.

Table 7.4, with *interest rates* held constant, suggests that government non-wage expenditure had a greater effect on *employment* than did personal income tax cuts (for the same effect on the budget balance) for all these countries except Italy, for which the two effects were identical.

There are thus a few differences in the ranking of these two measures according to the assumption made about monetary policy: but it remains true that, over the five years as a whole, for the clear majority of cases government non-wage expenditures had the greater effect on employment of these two fiscal measures for the same effect on the budget deficit. In no case was the ranking of these two measures in respect to their effects on *employment* reversed with the change in assumption about monetary policy.

The conclusion about the relative ranking of these two measures in terms of their effect on employment is thus consistent with the conclusion about their effect on real GDP if monetary policy is assumed to be used to hold interest rates constant (that is, to be 'accommodating'); whereas in the simulations with a fixed money supply we saw that the ranking of their relative effects on *real GDP* was generally the reverse of that for their effects on employment, except for the US, for which country government non-wage expenditures had the larger effect on both employment and real GDP under either assumption about monetary policy.

Table 5.3 showed that, with a fixed quantity of money, for each of these seven countries other than Germany and Italy (for each of which the effect was the same for each of the two instruments) government non-wage expenditures increased prices (the GDP price index) to a greater extent than did income tax cuts over the five years simulated.

Table 7.5 shows that, with *interest rates* held constant, again government non-wage expenditure increased the average price level over the five years to a greater extent than did cuts in personal income tax having the same effect on the government's financial balance for all seven countries, including Italy (for which country the reverse was true when the *money supply* was assumed to be held fixed).

It may thus be seen that, except for Italy, the ranking of these two fiscal measures in terms of their effects on the price level was the same whether it is the money supply or interest rates that are assumed to be held fixed by monetary policy.

It may be seen from Table 7.6 that, with interest rates held constant, for all seven countries a cut in personal income tax had a greater upward or smaller downward effect on net wealth than did government non-wage expenditure (or in some cases a positive effect where government expenditure had a negative effect). This is consistent with the ranking in Table 6.1, which showed that, with the quantity of money held fixed, personal income tax cuts had a smaller downward effect on net wealth than did government non-wage expenditure (or, in one case, an upward effect when government non-wage expenditure reduced it).

Table 7.4: Simulated effects on employment of government non-wage expenditure and personal income tax cuts in the seven major OECD countries, with interest rates held constant by monetary policy
(Average change in employment over five years as % of baseline, for a change over that period in the government's financial balance equal to 1% of GDP; with change in relation to rise in budget deficit equal to 1% of GDP in first year in parentheses)

	Rise in government non-wage expenditure	Cut in personal income tax
US	1.36 (4.86)	1.25 (3.89)
Japan	0.53 (2.11)	0.41 (1.67)
Germany	2.22 (6.37)	1.57 (4.89)
France	0.27 (1.58)	0.22 (1.18)
UK	0.84 (4.00)	0.67 (3.11)
Italy	0.11 (0.69)	0.11 (0.64)
Canada	0.84 (3.44)	0.48 (2.33)

Source: as for Table 7.3.

Table 7.5: Simulated effects on average GDP price index of changes in government non-wage expenditure and personal income tax cuts over five years in the seven major OECD countries, with floating exchange rates and interest rates held constant by monetary policy
(%ge point change for a rise in the budget deficit equal to 1% of GDP)

	Rise in government non-wage expenditure	Cut in personal income tax
US	5.72	4.56
Japan	1.64	1.16
Germany	2.39	1.68
France	0.51	0.32
UK	2.56	1.71
Italy	0.47	0.38
Canada	2.62	1.20

Source: as for Table 7.3.

*Table 7.6: Simulated effects of two fiscal measures upon net wealth in
the seven major OECD countries, with interest rates held constant
and floating exchange rates*
(%ge change as a ratio of GDP for a change in the budget
deficit equal to 1% of GDP)
'A'=Government non-wage expenditure; 'B'=Personal income tax cuts

| | Private investment | | Real foreign balance | | 'Net wealth' | |
	'A'	'B'	'A'	'B'	'A'	'B'
US	0.97	0.81	−1.04	−0.60	−0.07	+0.21
Japan	0.80	0.83	−0.58	−0.41	+0.22	+0.42
Germany	0.88	0.99	−1.26	−0.93	−0.38	+0.06
France	0.37	0.52	−0.34	−0.31	+0.03	+0.21
UK	0.39	0.34	−0.69	−0.55	−0.30	−0.21
Italy	0.23	0.43	−0.22	−0.04	+0.01	+0.39
Canada	0.52	0.31	−0.68	−0.07	−0.16	+0.24

Source: as for Table 7.3.

THE RELEVANCE OF EXCHANGE RATE POLICY

The extent to which the exchange rate is left free to vary with a change in
fiscal policy may also have a bearing on the relative effect of different fiscal
measures.

Simulations with fixed exchange rates may not appear to be very relevant
in the contemporary world; but if some greater degree of exchange rate fixity
in Europe is likely to occur in future, perhaps for those countries at least one
could argue that the assumption of fixed exchange rates may once again come
to have some relevance.

On the other hand, it should be borne in mind that fixity of an exchange
rate within a limited area such as Western Europe does not constitute overall
exchange rate fixity; for the more a currency is fixed in terms of its near
neighbours, the greater the extent of its fluctuations in terms of currencies
outside the group. It could perhaps be argued that when a very high proportion
of the country's trade and other payments is with the neighbours whose
currencies are relatively fixed in terms of its own, this situation is closer to
one of exchange rate fixity than to one of floating exchange rates. The
relevant situation for many European countries may, in any event, come to
be one that is intermediate between a floating exchange rate and one that is
fixed in terms of other currencies.

To that extent it is of some interest to ask whether the ranking of the two
fiscal instruments in terms of their effects on major macroeconomic objectives

is altered if exchange rates are kept (relatively) fixed, and, with the exchange rate fixed, what difference is made according to whether monetary policy is assumed to be accommodating or 'non-accommodating' (in these simulations, meaning that the quantity of money is held fixed by central bank action).

Relevance of the Degree of Exchange Rate Flexibility

On the assumption of a non-accommodating monetary policy – that is, that interest rates are left free to fall after government outlays are reduced – if the exchange rate is also left free to vary, one would expect this to provide some offsetting stimulus and strengthen the current account balance (further) as a result of the cut in government outlays. For the fall in imports resulting from the downward impact on demand that would result from the fall in government outlays would be reinforced by the tendency for the consequent fall in interest rates to reduce capital inflow, and so to weaken the exchange rate through the capital account, causing a depreciation, and thus some further fall in imports and rise in exports (compared with the fixed exchange rate situation). On the other hand, the direct effect of the cut in government outlays on the exchange rate through the tendency for the fall in aggregate demand would be in the direction of appreciation. It is an empirical matter which of these two effects on the exchange rate would predominate – or, indeed, whether they might more or less balance one another.

One set of simulations with models of different countries, assembled at the OECD in the 1980s (Chan-Lee and Kato, 1984) suggests that in the majority of those countries, at any rate after the first year (and for the US after the second year), the effect on real GDP (downwards in the case of a cut in government non-wage spending) is greater if the exchange rate is left floating than if it is kept fixed. In a substantial minority of the countries covered, however, there is a balance in the other direction – notably for the UK and Canada. These differences may well be merely the result of differences between the assumptions of the different models used in different countries; but, if there are significant real differences, one possible explanation is that capital account effects are especially important for countries with large international capital markets – the US (during the first two years), Britain and Canada (for which country the effects are much the same under fixed or floating rates for the first two years, with the current account effects on the currency apparently causing the countervailing expansionary effect to dominate in the third and fourth years). But it is not surprising if the (expansionary) capital account effects turn out to be more important mainly in countries that are subject to large and interest-sensitive international capital flows. (Simulations of income tax cuts with alternative settings of monetary policy are not available from this source.)

Table 7.7: Simulated effects on real GDP of two fiscal measures in seven major OECD countries with fixed and floating exchange rates and a fixed money supply (%ge change in real GDP for 1% of GDP rise in government borrowing, average of five years)

	Rise in government non-wage expenditure		Cut in personal income tax	
	Floating	Fixed	Floating	Fixed
US	0.56	3.16	0.69	0.69
Japan	0.58	0.56	0.56	0.56
Germany	0.69	0.61	0.70	0.63
France	0.48	0.45	0.53	0.51
UK	0.38	0.32	0.39	0.36
Italy	0.39	0.39	0.47	0.46
Canada	0.31	0.28	0.29	0.29

Source: as for Table 7.3.

Drawing upon the OECD simulations for the seven major countries made in the mid-1980s, Table 7.7 shows the simulated effects on real GDP of increases in government non-wage expenditure and income tax cuts over five years with both floating (reproduced from Table 3.3) and fixed exchange rates. It will be seen that this simulation suggests that there would be little or no difference in the effects of the two measures on real GDP according to whether exchange rates are fixed or floating, except for the US, for which country government non-wage expenditures have (on this evidence) a much greater effect with fixed than with floating exchange rates.

In Japan, government non-wage expenditure had the same effect as income tax cuts, under both fixed and floating exchange rates.

Table 7.8 shows that, over five years, whether exchange rates are fixed or floating, with *interest rates* held fixed, for all these countries except Italy, government non-wage expenditure has a greater effect on real GDP than personal income tax cuts for the same effect on the budget balance. This result contrasts with those where it was the quantity of money that was held constant, for (as Table 7.7 showed) in that case personal income tax cuts had a somewhat greater effect in five of the seven countries.

We saw in Table 3.3 that, *with a fixed money supply and floating exchange rates*, over a five-year period changes in personal income tax had a greater effect on real GDP than did changes in government non-wage expenditures for five of the seven countries (but not for the US and Canada).

Table 7.8: Simulated effects on real GDP of seven major OECD countries with fixed and floating exchange rates and fixed interest rates
(%ge change in real GDP for 1% of GDP rise in government borrowing, average of five years)

	Rise in government non-wage expenditure		Cut in personal income tax	
	Floating	Fixed	Floating	Fixed
US	2.60	2.04	2.29	2.00
Japan	2.47	2.22	2.05	1.87
Germany	0.69	2.08	0.70	1.83
France	0.85	0.83	0.80	0.78
UK	2.23	1.02	1.07	0.89
Italy	0.56	0.55	0.64	0.64
Canada	1.40	0.95	0.82	0.66

Source: as for Table 7.3.

Table 7.9: Simulated effects on unemployment and employment in seven major OECD countries of two fiscal instruments with a fixed exchange rate and a fixed money supply
(Effect over three years in parentheses)

	Effect on unemployment rate (percentage points)		%ge effect on employment	
	Government non-wage expenditures	Cut in personal income tax	Government non-wage expenditures	Cut in personal income tax
US	−0.21 (−0.41)	−0.22 (−0.32)	0.23 (0.44)	0.31 (0.46)
Japan	0.00 (0.00)	0.00 (0.00)	0.13 (0.19)	0.12 (0.16)
Germany	−0.15 (−0.37)	−0.15 (−0.26)	0.33 (0.44)	0.30 (0.30)
France	−0.11 (−0.10)	−0.11 (−0.08)	0.18 (0.17)	0.15 (0.30)
UK	−0.27 (−0.36)	−0.20 (−0.25)	0.38 (0.45)	0.27 (0.31)
Italy	−0.09 (−0.10)	−0.09 (−0.07)	0.08 (0.10)	0.11 (0.12)
Canada	−0.19 (−0.35)	−0.15 (−0.20)	0.22 (0.46)	0.23 (0.29)

The simulation used is that for a fixed money supply (a non-accommodating monetary policy) and fixed exchange rates.

Source: as for Table 7.3.

We saw in Table 7.3, however, that if *interest rates* are held constant, with floating exchange rates, for all these countries except Italy, government non-wage expenditure increases *real GDP* by less than personal income tax cuts for a given effect on the budget balance (whether one considers the effect on the budget balance over the whole five years or only that in the first year).

These various comparisons therefore suggest that for these two fiscal instruments – government non-wage expenditures and personal income tax cuts – even the ranking of the instruments in terms of their effects on real GDP and (as a comparison of Table 7.9 with Table 4.3 shows) on employment or unemployment may vary according to whether the exchange rate is fixed or floating, and whether one assumes that monetary policy is set so as to keep interest rates, or the money supply, constant.

It may be seen from Table 7.10 that this simulation with fixed interest rates and a fixed exchange rate also suggests that personal income tax cuts reduce wealth less than does a rise in government expenditure (or, in some cases, income tax cuts have a positive effect on wealth when government non-wage expenditure has a negative or zero effect). Government non-wage expenditure has a greater effect in moving the current account balance in the direction of deficit than a cut in personal income tax having the same effect on the budget balance, with a fixed exchange rate (and with either of the two assumptions about monetary policy). This conclusion was true also under the assumption of floating exchange rates and a fixed money supply (Table 7.4) or with floating exchange rates and a fixed money supply (with the exception of Canada, and for Italy, where the two instruments had identical effects). (See Table 6.1.)

Table 7.10: Simulated effects on net wealth in the seven major OECD countries of two fiscal instruments with fixed exchange rates and fixed interest rates
(Change from baseline as a %ge of GDP)
'A'=Government non-wage expenditure; 'B'=Personal income tax cuts

	Private investment		Real foreign balance		'Net wealth'	
	'A'	'B'	'A'	'B'	'A'	'B'
US	0.80	0.74	−1.21	−0.76	−0.41	−0.02
Japan	0.73	0.74	−0.73	−0.50	0.00	+0.24
Germany	0.70	0.91	−1.31	−1.07	−0.61	−0.15
France	0.37	0.46	−0.41	−0.32	−0.04	+0.14
UK	0.34	0.31	−0.82	−0.66	−0.52	−0.35
Italy	0.21	0.39	−0.28	−0.26	−0.07	+0.13
Canada	0.38	0.26	−0.82	−0.49	−0.44	−0.23

Source: as for Table 7.3.

Table 7.11: Simulated effects on net wealth in the seven major OECD countries of two fiscal instruments with fixed exchange rates and a fixed money supply
(Change from baseline as a %ge of GDP)
'A'=Government non-wage expenditure; 'B'=Personal income tax cuts

	Private investment		Real foreign balance		'Net wealth'	
	'A'	'B'	'A'	'B'	'A'	'B'
US	−0.06	−0.00	−0.46	−0.28	−0.52	−0.29
Japan	0.11	−0.00	−0.18	0.17	−0.29	−0.04
Germany	0.09	0.27	−0.46	−0.44	−0.37	−0.17
France	0.14	0.26	−0.24	−0.22	−0.10	+0.04
UK	−0.11	−0.05	−0.27	−0.24	−0.37	−0.29
Italy	0.08	0.23	−0.20	−0.20	−0.12	−0.04
Canada	0.09	0.09	−0.32	−0.24	−0.23	−0.15

Source: as for Table 7.3.

With almost no exceptions, therefore, the change of assumption about monetary policy and exchange rate policy does not significantly affect the ranking of these two instruments for these seven countries in respect of their effects on either the real foreign balance or net wealth.

CONCLUSION

Releasing the assumption of floating exchange rates does not change the general conclusion that increases in government non-wage expenditures have, in most cases, a more negative or smaller positive effect on net wealth (including both private investment and the current account balance). But the conclusion that, over a period of five years, with floating exchange rates and a fixed quantity of money, government non-wage expenditure has less effect than personal income tax cuts in increasing real output or raising employment may or may not continue to be true for a particular country if exchange rates are held fixed or if interest rates are fixed by monetary policy under floating exchange rates. Under each of the sets of assumptions about monetary policy and exchange rate policy, however, government non-wage expenditure appears (on this evidence) to be more inflationary than cuts in personal income tax.

This implies that if a government tries to reduce a budget deficit by cutting government non-wage expenditure it will have a bigger downward effect on inflation, and a bigger upward effect on net wealth than if it raised personal income tax, whatever assumption one makes about monetary policy or exchange rate policy.

One cannot be sure, however (on the basis of the evidence considered above), that the ranking of these two instruments will remain the same in terms of their effects on real GDP or employment and unemployment irrespective of the assumptions made about monetary policy and exchange rate policy. To judge from the simulations for the whole OECD area, however – which are not available with alternative assumptions about exchange rates – a change of the assumption about monetary policy from accommodating to non-accommodating does not alter the conclusion drawn from those simulations that *a package of direct taxation* (including employers' social security contributions) has a greater downward effect on employment and real GDP than does a cut in government non-wage expenditure. In view of the difference made to the conclusions on these effects relating to personal income tax cuts alone, which appear to differ from the ranking of direct taxation generally compared with government non-wage expenditure, one could conclude from this limited evidence that the likely explanation is that employers' social security contributions (in effect a tax on labour) continue to have a greater effect in reducing real output or employment than do reductions in government non-wage expenditure, whatever assumptions one might make about monetary policy and the exchange rate.

If the aim is expansion with a minimum upward effect on the budget deficit, government non-wage expenditures seem on this evidence likely to have the disadvantage over personal income tax cuts (and presumably also over cuts in a range of direct taxation) that they will increase inflation to a greater extent, and will have a larger downward effect on net wealth than cuts in personal income tax, whether exchange rates are floating or fixed.

Moreover, if the government wishes to keep the current account as strong as possible and also reduce the budget deficit, it would do better to reduce the budget deficit by cutting non-wage government expenditures than by raising personal income taxation. Again, this conclusion appears to be generally true whether exchange rates are assumed to be fixed or floating.

Finally, it should be emphasised that the ranking of government non-wage expenditures compared with personal income tax cuts in terms of their relative effects on the various macroeconomic objectives may not give an indication of the ranking of other types of government expenditure or other types of taxation. In particular, as we saw in Chapter 6, one could reasonably expect that government investment expenditure would do more to increase national net wealth than government non-wage outlays in general, and probably more than most types of tax cuts.

The most that one could conclude from the limited amount of evidence assembled in this chapter is that the particular assumptions that are made about the setting of monetary policy and about exchange rate policy are more likely to affect the ranking of instruments in terms of their effects on real output or employment than their effects on inflation or (private) net wealth, including the current account balance.

8 Effects of Different Combinations of Fiscal Measures

Previous chapters have considered, separately, some evidence relating to comparisons of the effects on various macroeconomic objectives of different types of taxation, and also of different types of government outlays.

The present chapter draws these threads together by looking at the policy implications for various macroeconomic objectives of different combinations of various taxes with one another and also with various types of government outlays.

Effects on Output, Inflation and Net Wealth

We saw in Tables 3.1 and 3.2 that, for the OECD as a whole, over a period of five years a change in direct taxation had a greater effect on output than did a rise of the same size in government non-wage expenditure. Table 3.3 showed that personal income tax cuts had a greater effect on output than rises in government non-wage expenditure for five of the seven major OECD countries (the exceptions being Japan – for which country the two effects were the same – and Canada): but in simulations with individual country models (Table 3.4) the reverse appeared to be true (see Table 8.3).

We saw in Chapter 5 that, in all these simulations, government non-wage outlays had a greater upward effect on prices than personal income tax cuts, except for the OECD simulation for Germany and Italy, where the effects of the two instruments on prices was in each of these two cases the same. The results from the OECD simulations for the seven major countries are summarised in Table 8.1. (As the OECD Interlink model takes account of repercussions operating through other countries, it seems preferable to take the results of those simulations as a guide, rather than those shown in Table 8.3 with individual country models.)

The third column of this table puts these two effects together, showing that for every one of these seven countries government non-wage expenditures had a greater upward effect on prices than did personal income tax cuts *for a given stimulus to the level of real GDP.*

Table 8.1: Simulated effects on various macroeconomic objectives of government non-wage expenditure and personal income tax cuts for the seven major OECD countries
(%ge points change for a rise in financial deficit equal to 1% of GDP/GNP, five-year average)
'A'=Government non-wage expenditure; 'B'=Personal income tax cuts

	Price level		Level of real GDP				'Net wealth'*			
	(1)		(2)		(3)=(1)/(2)		(4)		(5)=(4)/(2)	
	'A'	'B'	'A'	'B'	'A'	'B'	'A'	'B'	'A'	'B'
US	1.33	1.13	0.58	0.69	2.29	1.64	−0.48	−0.27	−0.83	−0.39
Japan	0.37	0.30	0.58	0.58	0.64	0.52	−0.44	−0.22	−0.76	−0.38
Germany	0.25	0.20	0.69	0.70	0.36	0.29	−0.48	−0.24	−0.70	−0.34
France	0.14	0.10	0.48	0.53	0.29	0.19	−0.17	+0.01	−0.35	+0.02
UK	0.18	0.09	0.38	0.39	0.47	0.23	−0.45	−0.33	−1.16	−0.85
Italy	0.20	0.16	0.39	0.47	0.51	0.34	−0.11	+0.01	−0.28	+0.02
Canada	0.75	0.49	0.31	0.29	2.42	1.69	−0.23	−0.16	−0.74	−0.55

* Change in real current account balance plus change in private investment as a %ge of GDP.

The simulations assume a fixed money supply and floating exchange rate.

Source: Derived from Richardson (1987).

The figures in column (3) imply that for all these countries, a reduction in government non-wage expenditures would bring a better combination of inflation and real output than a rise in personal income taxation having the same effect on the budget deficit.

If a government is concerned with avoiding a fall in real GDP resulting from a reduction in the budget deficit over a five-year period, it could (on this evidence), in most of these countries, do so by reducing non-wage government expenditure and reducing personal income tax by something less. For the US, for example, a cut in government non-wage expenditures equal to 1% of GDP, offset by a cut in personal income tax of anything more than about 0.8% of GDP, but less than 1% of GDP, would on these figures raise the level of real GDP while also reducing the budget deficit. Over a three-year period, however, government non-wage expenditures appear, on the balance of the evidence, to have a greater effect on real GDP or (in most of the countries) employment than a cut in personal income tax having the same effect on the budget balance. Over the shorter period, therefore, personal income tax would have to be cut by more than government outlays if a fall in real GDP were to be avoided; and a *rise* in government spending accompanied by a slightly greater rise in income tax could stimulate output while reducing the budget deficit.

Column (5) shows that government non-wage outlays had the larger downward effect on net wealth (private investment plus the change in the current account deficit) for a given stimulus to the level of real GDP. It should, however, be borne in mind that if the government outlays had been on investment, for a rise in this category equal to 1% of GDP, the effect of the government outlays on net wealth, including publicly owned capital, would have been positive in each case.

As government non-wage outlays have for the US (on the figures in Table 8.1) nearly twice as great a downward effect on private net wealth as do personal income tax cuts, a reduction in the budget deficit brought about by a rise in government outlays of, say, 1% and a rise in personal taxation of more than 1% but less than about 1.8% of GDP – thus reducing the budget deficit – in the US would have a *downward* effect on net wealth. One should, however, bear in mind that if the government expenditures were on investment goods, the resulting rise in public investment should also be taken into account in measuring the effect upon total national net wealth.

The foregoing arguments imply that, in the US over a five-year period, a cut in personal income tax just over 0.8% (but less than 1%) of GDP accompanied by a cut in government non-wage expenditures equal to 1% of GDP would raise the level of real GDP and reduce prices, as well as stimulating net wealth, while also reducing the budget deficit.

Table 8.2: Simulated effects on current account balance of government expenditure and income tax cuts for 1% rise in growth rate of real GDP in the seven major OECD countries
(%ge of GDP)

	US	Japan	Germany	France	UK	Italy	Canada
Rise in government non-wage expenditure	–0.75	–0.58	–0.83	–0.65	–0.97	–0.49	–1.04
Income tax cut	–0.38	–0.45	–0.77	–0.51	–0.79	–0.40	–0.90

Source: As for Table 8.1.

Table 8.2 shows the relative effect of these two instruments on the current account balance for a 1% rise in the level of real GDP for each of these seven countries. (The effect on the current account is included in that for the effects on net wealth in Table 8.1.)

If a government were concerned about the state of the current account balance, it could, for any of these countries, find a combination of cuts in government outlays coupled with smaller cuts in personal income tax that would strengthen the current account balance while in most cases increasing the level of real GDP.

Summarising the implications of the results drawn upon in Table 8.1 for a policy directed towards reducing the budget deficit, therefore, it may be concluded that if that were done by increases in personal income tax accompanied by a slightly smaller simultaneous rise in government non-wage expenditures this could have an upward effect on prices for any given level of real GDP, a downward effect on employment and national wealth (moving the current account balance in the direction of deficit) and also (for all of them except Germany and Italy – for each of which the two measures have the same effect) a downward effect on the level of real GDP. This means that a reduction in the budget deficit that took the form of a cut in government non-wage expenditures and a slightly smaller cut in personal income tax could reduce prices, increase net wealth (strengthening the current account balance) and raise the rate of growth of real GDP for all of them except Germany and Italy.

Table 8.3 shows the results of simulations using some individual country models. These results confirm the evidence in earlier tables that government non-wage expenditures are more inflationary than personal tax cuts for a given effect on the budget deficit; and also that government outlays move the current account in the direction of deficit more than does an equivalent income tax cut.

Table 8.3: Simulated effects on various macroeconomic objectives of
government non-wage expenditures and personal income tax cuts for
five major OECD countries
(%ge change, average of Years 1, 2, 3 & 7, for 1% of GDP rise in
budget deficit in first year)
'A' = Government non-wage expenditure; 'B' = Personal income tax cuts

	Real GDP (1)		Price level (2)		(3) = (2)/(1)		Current account (4)	
	'A'	'B'	'A'	'B'	'A'	'B'	'A'	'B'
US	0.89	0.82	0.52	0.35	0.58	0.43	–3.91	–2.82
Japan	2.35	1.41	1.13	0.69	0.48	0.49	–1.32	–0.55
France	1.62	0.65	0.65	0.00	0.40	0.00	–8.14	–4.09
UK	0.80	0.56	1.17	–0.35	1.46	–0.62	–1.15	–1.11
Canada 1	0.55	0.57	0.61	0.59	1.11	1.04	–3.08	–3.43
Canada 2	1.74	1.00	0.50	0.69	0.29	0.69	–3.06	–3.03

Monetary policy is assumed to be non-accommodating.

Source: Derived from Chan-Lee and Kato (1984).

But, in apparent contrast to the OECD simulations for major countries reported in Table 8.1, these simulations using individual country models suggest that government non-wage expenditures have a *greater* effect on real GDP for a given effect on the budget deficit (in this case, the change in the budget deficit in the first year) than do personal income tax cuts; but, as in these simulations drawn upon in Table 8.3 the effects can be related only to the change in the budget deficit in the first year (changes in the budget in subsequent years not being given), they are more nearly comparable to the figures in parentheses in Table 3.3 for the seven major countries, which similarly related the effects to the change in the budget in the first year. Those, too, showed government non-wage outlays as having, on this measure, a greater effect on real GDP than personal income tax cuts. (This illustrates that the relative effect of two measures in relation to government borrowing in the year of the change may differ from that in relation to the change in government borrowing over a longer period.)

Moreover, in these simulations with individual country models also, government non-wage expenditure has a greater effect in moving the current account towards deficit for a given stimulus to real GDP than does a cut in personal income tax, for all countries covered except for one of the two models for Canada. The conclusions from Table 8.2 on this point are thus confirmed by this very different set of simulations.

Table 8.3 also suggests that (again, with the exception of one of the models for Canada) government non-wage outlays have a greater upward effect on prices than cuts in personal income taxation. But that does not indicate that a rise in government non-wage outlays (still less a rise in *all* government outlays) is, over the five years, more inflationary (in this sense), than are *any* types of tax cut; though the simulations for the UK and those for the EEC summarised below strongly suggest that household income tax cuts are the most inflationary of the three *tax cut* measures simulated; indeed, that cuts in VAT and taxes on employment (employers' social security contributions or national insurance contributions), the two other types of tax cut simulated, are more likely to *reduce* inflation.

The various results drawn upon in some earlier simulations (especially Tables 3.12, 3.13 and 3.15) suggest that government expenditure on *wage* items has a clearly greater effect on real GDP than non-wage expenditure and also greater than cuts in personal income tax of the same size, and perhaps greater than cuts in direct taxation generally (inclusive of social security contributions).

Table 8.4: Simulated effects on rate of inflation and level of real GDP of whole OECD of changes in government non-wage expenditures and cuts in a package of direct taxation
(%ge points change, five-year average)

	Rate of inflation (1)	Real GDP (level) (2)	(3)=(1)/(2)
Government non-wage expenditure	−0.09	1.2	−0.07
Cut in direct taxation	−0.49	2.1	−0.23

The simulation used is that with unchanged real interest rates.

Source: Derived from Richardson et al. (1994).

Table 8.4 shows results from a simulation for the whole of the OECD. There are are important differences between the types of tax changes assumed in this simulation and those drawn upon in previous tables. This OECD simulation for tax changes includes not only personal income tax but also employers' social security or national insurance contributions. This simulation of increases in direct taxation for the OECD suggests that government non-wage spending was much more inflationary for a given effect in increasing real GDP than cuts in the package of direct taxation simulated there. The table also implies that a cut in government non-wage outlays of, say, 1% of GDP could be accompanied by a cut in direct taxation of something over 0.6% (but less than 1%) of GDP and still leave a net stimulus to real GDP while reducing the budget deficit over a five-year period.

EVIDENCE FOR THE US

Table 8.5 brings together results from the McKibbin and Bagnoli (Computable General Equilibrium) model simulations for the US with certain other simulations for the US reported in earlier chapters.

The comparison of indirect tax cuts with cuts in personal income tax is especially striking. Cuts in indirect taxation reduce inflation, stimulate growth and employment, and have a much smaller downward effect on net wealth than do personal income tax cuts, either those directed mainly at higher income groups (in the McKibbin and Bagnoli simulations) or the more general ones in the Richardson simulations of the mid-1980s (shown in the bottom line of the table).

This means that a shift from indirect taxation to personal income taxation could be expected, on these figures, to stimulate growth, reduce unemployment and increase net wealth; while a rise in personal income taxation rather greater than the cut in indirect taxation could be expected to have these desirable effects on the main macroeconomic objectives, while also reducing the budget deficit.

Table 8.5: Simulated effects of different fiscal measures on various macroeconomic objectives in the US for an increase in the budget deficit equal to 1% of GDP

(%ge deviation from trend relative to deviation of budget deficit from trend as percentage of GDP over first five years)

	Employment (1)	GDP (2)	Inflation (3)	'Net wealth' (4)	Inflation/ GDP (5)=(3)/(2)
Permanent investment tax credit	1.86	3.32	−0.21	+3.10	−0.06
Temporary investment tax credit	1.16	2.38	0.89	+2.17	0.37
Permanent labour tax credit	2.19	1.88	−0.28	+0.04	−0.15
Cut in indirect tax	2.75	1.69	−1.52	−0.14	−0.90
Temporary labour tax credit	1.36	1.07	0.75	−0.07	0.70
Corporation tax cut	0.65	0.94	0.03	+0.46	0.03
Government infrastructure investment (cut-off)	0.17	0.82	0.19	+0.71	0.23
Government infrastructure investment (gradual)	0.66	0.75	0.18	+0.09	0.24
Lump-sum transfers to households	0.48	0.36	−0.24	0.19	−0.67
Government non-investment spending	0.52	0.56	0.09	−0.11	0.16
Income tax cut	0.53	0.20	0.14	−0.26	0.70
Memorandum items					
Non-wage public spending	0.23	0.58	0.47	−0.48	0.81
Cut in personal income tax	0.31	0.69	0.43	−0.27	0.62
Rise in public spending*	n.a.	1.56	1.30	(0.42)	0.83
Cut in direct taxation*	n.a.	0.81	0.72	(0.29)	0.89

'n.a.' signifies 'not available'.
'Net wealth'= effect on private investment plus or minus effect on trade balance.
*Average of Years 1 and 5. Figures in parentheses for current account balance.

Source: Derived from graphical data in McKibbin and Bagnoli (1993), and from data supplied by them; for memorandum items, Richardson (1987) and Knoester (1988).

For example, a rise in personal income tax (on the results of the simulation towards the end) would increase net wealth by about twice as much as a cut of the same order in indirect taxation would reduce it. A cut of just over 0.5% (but less than 1%) of GDP in indirect taxation coupled with a rise of about 1% of GDP in income tax would thus leave a net upward effect on net wealth. There would also be a substantial net stimulus to real GDP and employment on those figures; and both the cut in indirect tax and the rise in personal income tax would reduce inflation over the period under discussion.

The obverse of these propositions is that if the attempt to reduce the budget deficit took the form mainly of increases in indirect taxation, this could be expected to have net adverse effects on all the main macroeconomic objectives, but that increases in personal income taxation would be likely to have less by way of adverse effects on the various macroeconomic objectives. Increases in direct taxation with cuts in indirect taxation would be available that would reduce the budget deficit while also having favourable effects on the main macroeconomic objectives.

EVIDENCE FOR THE EEC

The conclusions in the preceding section about the effects on inflation of different types of taxation in the US are consistent with those reached in the simulation for the then EEC by the secretariat of the EEC some years ago, to the effect that increases in VAT – and also increases in social security contributions – tend to increase inflation in subsequent years (five years being covered in the simulations), whereas increases in income tax tend to reduce it, though probably to a smaller extent than reductions in government consumption or investment. The balance of evidence from the University of Warwick simulations for the UK (discussed below) also suggests that VAT and employers' national insurance contributions tended to exert upward pressure on prices (at least for period of up to five years); whereas increases in income tax, and cuts in government spending, tended to reduce it. For the majority of these models, cuts in government non-wage expenditures would have a greater downward effect on prices for a given reduction over the period in real GDP than a rise in personal income tax having the same effect on the budget deficit. For all of the models, a cut in government non-wage expenditures would have a greater effect in strengthening the current account balance than would an equal rise in personal income tax.

Table 8.6 draws on the results of the simulation for the EEC as it was in the mid-1980s.

If the aim of a government is to raise real GDP and reduce unemployment without increasing inflation, clearly the most appropriate measure, on those figures, would be to reduce employers' national insurance or social security contributions; and the next most appropriate measure of those simulated would be a cut in household indirect taxation. On this criterion, a cut in household direct taxation would be the least appropriate form of stimulus. But if account has to be taken of the effects on the country's net wealth (or on the current account taken alone) increases in government consumption would be the least appropriate measure of those in the table.

By the same token, on the figures from this EEC simulation, if a government is aiming to reduce its budget deficit with as small a reduction in real GDP as possible, and as large a reduction in inflation as possible, the least appropriate means would be an increase in employers' social security contributions, followed by indirect tax increases. On this criterion, it would be more appropriate to increase household direct taxation or to reduce government outlays.

Table 8.6: Simulated effects of different fiscal measures on various macroeconomic objectives in EEC for a rise in budget deficit equal to 1% of GDP (%ge points change five-year average)

	Growth rate of real GDP (1)	Unemploy-ment (2)	Inflation (3)	Net wealth (4)	(5) =(3)/(1)
Cut in employers' social security contributions	0.20	−1.72	−0.30	+0.41	−1.50
Cut in indirect taxation	0.34	−1.12	−0.16	−0.04	−0.47
Rise in public consumption	0.14	−0.31	0.49	−1.54	3.50
Rise in public investment	0.14	−0.31	0.49	−0.54	3.50
Cut in household direct taxation	0.19	−0.30	0.27	−0.21	1.42

Source: Derived from Dramais (1986).

An example of a mix that would reduce the budget deficit but stimulate output would be a cut in employers' national insurance contributions equal to 1% of GDP and a reduction in public consumption equal to anything more than 1% of GDP but less than about 1.4% of GDP. Each of these two measures would also tend to increase net wealth.

These figures imply that a government wishing to reduce its budget deficit with a minimal downward effect on net wealth would do better to reduce its own consumption (though not its own investment), or perhaps to raise household direct taxation, rather than to raise either of the other two taxes simulated here.

EVIDENCE FOR BELGIUM

One simulation for an individual small country for which indicators of the effects on all the main macroeconomic objectives of several fiscal instruments are available is that for Belgium (Bogaert et al., 1990).

It may be seen from Table 8.7 that, in terms of the effect on prices for a given stimulus to GDP, a cut in employers' social security contributions scores best, with a cut in VAT also reducing prices. But in terms of its stimulus to real GDP for a given rise in the budget deficit, a cut in VAT scores less highly than any measure apart from a cut in employers' social security contributions. As with the results for the EEC as a whole shown in Table 8.6, these were the two preferred measures in that they could provide a price-reducing stimulus to employment and output. The greatest stimulus to growth and reduction in unemployment results from public expenditure on employment, followed by state investment. State investment is also the only measure of stimulation that increases 'net wealth'.

Table 8.7: Simulated effects of different fiscal measures on various macroeconomic objectives for Belgium
(For a rise in budget deficit equal to 1% of GDP, five-year totals)

	Real GDP (1)	Unem-ployment (2)	Price level (%) (3)	'Net wealth' (4)	Prices/ GDP (5)=(3)/(1)
Rise in total employment in public sector	0.98	−14.23	1.30	−0.94	1.32
Rise in state investment	0.76	−2.45	0.09	+0.64	0.12
Rise in social security transfers to households	0.54	−2.09	0.18	−0.57	0.33
Cut in personal income tax	0.39	−1.53	0.13	−0.37	0.33
Cut in VAT on private consumption products	0.33	−14.56	−0.37	−0.53	−1.12
Cut in employers' social security contributions	0.13	−13.30	−4.68	−0.38	−36.00

*Deviation from baseline of gross capital formation plus change in net exports as a percentage of GNP.
'Price level' is the effect on the level of the consumption price index.

Source: Derived from Bogaert et al. (1990).

The implication is that reductions in the budget deficit that are brought about by cuts in public expenditure, especially that on employment and public investment, will have a greater downward effect on real GDP than any of the other measures; but that increases in VAT will increase unemployment more than any other measure simulated (for a given effect in reducing the budget deficit).

There is therefore no clear conclusion for Belgium from these figures about which measures it would be best to use to reduce the budget deficit: it will depend upon which of the various macroeconomic objectives the government considers most important. This evidence suggests that cuts in income tax and increases in social security transfers would do less to reduce unemployment than any of the other measures; and that a net cut in unemployment could be brought about at the same time as a cut in the budget deficit if a rise in income tax were accompanied by a somewhat smaller rise in government outlays on public investment or public employment. Indeed, increases in any of the taxes simulated here, if accompanied by appropriately smaller increases in either of the three forms of government outlay simulated, could be expected on these figures to lead to a rise in the rate of growth of real GDP and also a reduction of the budget deficit.

EVIDENCE FOR THE UK

Table 8.8 shows, for the UK, the simulated effect on the rate of inflation over the average of five years for each 1% stimulus to real GDP over the same period from various fiscal measures.

It may be seen that a government wishing to reduce the PSBR while achieving the best combination of inflation and real GDP (that is, the greatest downward effect on inflation for a given reduction in real GDP) would, on these figures, reduce government spending. An increase in income tax would be the preferred alternative in one model and equal first choice in another, but less likely to reduce inflation than would a cut in government outlays in the other four.

At the other extreme, an increase in VAT of the same size could be expected to make inflation worse, as well as reducing real GDP growth over the period. This evidence is inconclusive about the ranking of changes in employers' social security contributions: in two models an increase in these would make inflation worse as well as reducing real GDP, but in another two an increase in them would reduce inflation even more than reducing government outlays. In any case, the balance of this evidence suggests that an increase in national insurance contributions would either reduce inflation or increase it by less than a rise in VAT.

By the same token, therefore, a government wishing to give a stimulus to real GDP with the least possible increase in inflation (or, preferably, reducing it) would reduce VAT or, as a second choice, reduce national insurance contributions or perhaps income tax, rather than increase its own spending.

Table 8.8: Simulated effects on inflation in the UK for 1% stimulus to GDP from various fiscal measures
(Five-year average of change in rate of increase in consumer price index for 1% stimulus to real GDP)

	LBS	NIESR	HMT	BE	OEF	STR	Average	Median
Government spending	0.61	0.69	0.55	1.40	0.67	0.58	0.75	0.65
Income tax cuts	0.68	0.50	0.07	0.05	0.09	0.58	0.33	0.30
Cut in national insurance contributions	0.72	1.00	−0.94	0.67	−0.14	0.56	0.31	0.61
Cut in VAT	−2.56	0.46	−0.95	−0.07	−0.08	0.29	−0.48	−0.08

For key to models, see Table 3.8.

*Memorandum items**
Effect on GDP price index for 1% rise in real GDP
(Average of Years 1, 2, 3 and 7)

Government non-wage expenditure	1.46
Personal income tax cuts	0.62

Source for simulations with various models of the UK economy: Derived from Church et al. (1993).
* Memorandum items derived from Chan-Lee and Kato (1984) (in which monetary policy is assumed to be non-accommodating).

The implication is that there are (on this evidence) a number of combinations of these instruments that could reduce the PSBR while also stimulating real GDP. These would involve moving one of the instruments near the bottom of the table in an expansionary direction, while tightening up on one of the instruments that are higher in the table. If the instrument that was eased was VAT (and perhaps also, on some of the evidence, if it was a cut in national insurance contributions), combinations of these measures would be available that were expansionary in terms of their effect on real GDP, and which could also reduce the rate of inflation over the period – as both the cut in VAT and the rather greater cut in government spending or increase in income tax (required to reduce the PSBR) would reduce inflation.

Other simulations relating to the UK, among other countries (Chan-Lee and Kato, 1984, and Richardson, 1987), summarised in Tables 8.8 and 8.9, suggest that government non-wage expenditure is more inflationary than personal income tax cuts for a given stimulus to real GDP. Table 8.6 also suggested that, on the balance of that evidence for the EEC as a whole, *total* government expenditure (including wage expenditures, and therefore presumably close to the definition used in the University of Warwick simulations) was more inflationary than income tax cuts.

Putting together the evidence from these various simulations for the UK, one could conclude that government non-wage expenditures are probably more inflationary for a given stimulus to real GDP than total government expenditure, or that on wages alone, as well as being more inflationary for a given stimulus than personal income tax cuts. This would suggest that the greatest downward impact on inflation for a given downward effect on real output by the use of one of these instruments taken alone for reducing the PSBR would be cuts in government non-wage expenditure. But combinations of measures would be available that would reduce the PSBR while also stimulating output or employment; and some of those would actually reduce inflation.

Table 8.9: *Simulated effects on inflation in the UK of government non-wage expenditure and personal income tax cuts*
(%ge points change for 1% stimulus to real GDP)

	Real government expenditure	Personal income tax cuts
With interest rates held fixed	0.94	0.76
With money supply held fixed	0.19	0.12

Note: Both simulations assume floating exchange rates.

Source: Derived from Richardson (1987) and data supplied by him.

Effects on the Current Account Balance

Evidence for the UK relating to the effect of different fiscal measures on the country's net wealth is not available, but Table 8.10 shows the simulated effects of various fiscal measures on the current account balance for a given stimulus to real GDP. It does not, however, suggest a clear conclusion about whether for Britain government expenditure has a smaller upward effect on the current account balance (for a given rise in real GDP) than any of the forms of tax cuts simulated. On the average of the models, and in three of them individually, however, government expenditure has a smaller effect on the current account balance than either of the tax cuts. The results vary from model to model for the three types of tax cut simulated; but, on balance, the evidence implies that a cut in VAT has less effect in increasing the current account deficit than do either of the other two types of tax cut.

Table 8.10: Simulated effect on UK current account of various fiscal measures (Effect on current account balance in billion pounds sterling for 1% rise in GDP, over first five years)

	LBS	NIESR	HMT	BE*	OEF	STR	Average
Government expenditure*	−2.88	−3.36	−1.92	−1.50	−1.43	−2.29	−1.26
Income tax cuts	−2.71	−2.91	−3.80	−2.55	−2.12	−2.17	−2.71
Cut in VAT	−1.26	−3.62	−3.17	−1.97	−2.16	−2.36	−2.42
Cut in employers' national insurance contributions	−2.59	−4.79	−2.44	−2.06	−2.44	−2.45	−2.80

*Average of first four years.
Note: Nominal interest rates are assumed fixed.
For key to models see Table 3.12.

Source: Derived from Church et al. (1993).

Other simulations relating to the UK (among other countries) drawn upon in Tables 8.11 and 8.12 (Richardson, 1987 and Chan-Lee and Kato, 1984) provide ambiguous evidence for the UK about the relative ranking of government non-wage expenditures and personal income tax cuts in terms of their effects on the current account balance for a given stimulus to real GDP.

Table 8.11: Simulated effects of government non-wage expenditure and personal income tax cuts on current account of the UK for a 1% stimulus to real GDP (first five years

	Real GDP government expenditure	Personal income tax cuts
With fixed interest rates	−0.57	−0.51
With fixed money supply	−0.80	−0.96

Note: Both simulations assume floating exchange rates.

Source: Derived from Richardson (1987) and data supplied by him.

In marked contrast to the simulation (Richardson, 1987) with an accommodating monetary policy, in the University of Warwick simulations summarised in Table 8.10, which assume a fixed interest rate (an accommodating monetary policy) the balance of the evidence was that income tax cuts had a greater effect in increasing the current account deficit (for a given effect on real GDP) than did total government expenditure. But the sum of this evidence about the relative effect of these two measures upon the current account balance for a given effect on real GDP is inconclusive.

Table 8.12: Simulated effects of government non-wage expenditure and personal income tax cuts on UK current account balance for a 1% stimulus to real GDP
(As a %ge of GDP, average of Years 1 ,2, 3 & 7)

Real government expenditure	Cut in personal income tax
−1.43	−1.98

Note: This simulation assumes a non-accommodating monetary policy and floating exchange rates.

Source: Derived from Chan-Lee and Kato (1984).

EVIDENCE FOR FOUR NORDIC COUNTRIES

It is clear from the results of simulations for Nordic countries shown in Table 8.13 that in each case a cut in VAT reduced inflation over the five years after the change (and longer, according to results not used in the table, some of which extend to eleven years, one to ten, and one to seven years), while also increasing the rate of growth of real GDP over the period. Of the two other measures simulated, in each model the cut in local income tax had a greater upward effect on inflation for a given rise in real GDP than did a rise in government expenditure on employment. This result may be compared with those for other countries, or groups of countries, where government *non-wage* expenditure had a *greater* upward effect on inflation for a given rise in real GDP than a cut in either personal income tax (in most cases) or a range of direct taxes.

It appears (on the evidence for these countries considered in Chapters 3 and 4) that there are combinations of measures that would reduce the budget deficit while giving a stimulus to real GDP (and employment). For four of the models, this would consist of a rise in government expenditure on employment accompanied by a somewhat greater rise in local income tax: and for the other (ADAM – that relating to Denmark), it would consist of a cut in government expenditure on employment, accompanied by a smaller reduction in local income tax or VAT. (See Table 4.12.) (These simulations tell us nothing about government non-wage expenditures, for which we would have to consider evidence from other simulations such as those discussed above.)

Table 8.13: Simulated effect of various fiscal measures on price level in four Nordic countries for 1% increase in rate of growth of real GDP
(%ge change, average of Years 1, 2, 3 & 5)

Model:	ADAM	MODAG	KOSMOS	KESSU	BOF4
Government employment expenditure	1.37	0.20	0.92	0.02	0.39
Cut in local income tax	0.42	0.75	0.64	0.00	0.50
Cut in VAT	−1.52	−6.36	−4.24	−1.29	−2.01

For key to models see Table 3.12.
Note: It has been confirmed by the authors that the simulations they give for local income tax are in fact for a *reduction* (whereas the table in the original states that it was for an *increase*). The signs in this table are those for a reduction.

Source: Derived from Wallis and Whitley (1991).

Effects on the Current Account Balance

Figures are not available from the simulation for Nordic countries to estimate the effect of the various fiscal measures on 'net wealth', but only for the effects on the current account balance.

It is clear from Table 8.14 that, in four of the five models, a cut in VAT has a smaller effect in the direction of weakening the current account than either a cut in local income tax or a rise in government employment expenditure, for a given effect on real GDP. (The exception is Denmark, for which country a rise in government employment expenditure had the least effect.)

The evidence summarised in Table 8.14 suggests that if one aim is to minimise the increase in the current account deficit, a stimulus would best be given by cutting VAT, rather than by the other measures; and that a government (other than that of Denmark) wishing to reduce its budget deficit with as small a rise in the current account deficit as possible, and as much reduction in the rate of inflation as possible, would best do so by reductions in its employment expenditures or by increases in local income tax, and not by increases in VAT. (This conclusion agrees with the evidence considered earlier relating to the EEC as it was in the mid-1980s.) For Denmark, these figures suggest that if the stimulus were given by a rise in government employment expenditure and a slightly greater rise in one of these two taxes, that would reduce the budget deficit and strengthen the current account.

Table 8.14: Simulated effect of various fiscal measures on the current account
balance of four Nordic countries for a 1% rise in real GDP
(%ge of GDP)

Model:	ADAM	MODAG	KOSMOS	KESSU	BOF4
Rise in government employment expenditure	−0.90	−1.05	−0.68	−0.36	−0.38
Cut in local income tax	−2.06	−0.38	−0.61	−0.69	−0.21
Cut in VAT	−2.05	−0.25	−0.49	−0.23	−0.13

For key to models see Table 3.12.

Note: It has been confirmed by the authors that the simulations they give for local income tax are in fact for a *reduction* (whereas the table in the original states that it was for an *increase*). The signs in this table are those appropriate to a reduction.

Source: Derived from Wallis and Whitley (1991).

COMPARISONS OF POLICY CONCLUSIONS FROM DIFFERENT MODELS

The results from the various simulations considered above suggest some broad conclusions about the relative effects of changes in different forms of government outlay and revenue upon output and employment.

The most recent – the OECD simulation for government non-wage outlays and a range of *direct* taxation (considered in aggregate) concludes that cuts in government non-wage expenditures have less downward effect on employment or output than increases in direct taxation (income tax plus social security contributions) for a given effect on the budget balance. But we have seen that some simulations for Scandinavian countries, and also that for Belgium, indicate that for a given rise in the budget deficit government expenditure on employment has a greater effect – on both employment and output – than changes in the two types of taxation considered in those simulations. This may imply that government expenditures on employment have more effect on output and employment than do government non-wage expenditures. It could also imply that the range of direct taxation considered in the OECD simulation has more effect on output and employment than the income taxation considered in the simulations for the Scandinavian countries and Belgium. In the simulation for Belgium, it is clear that public employment expenditures have far more effect on real GDP than cuts in either income tax or indirect taxation (for the same effect on the budget balance). For Belgium, income tax cuts and government consumption expenditures, together with social security transfers, rank near the bottom of the list in terms of their effect on real GDP for a given effect on the budget balance.

Several other simulations relate to government expenditure generally (that is, without specifying that it is non-wage or employment expenditures separately). Those for the EEC imply that a rise in public investment has a smaller effect on real GDP for a given effect on the government's fiscal balance than do changes in indirect taxes or changes in employers' social security contributions, but a greater effect than that of changes in household direct taxation. This appears to be further evidence that one should view with caution the OECD writers' conclusions about the relative effects of changes in government outlays on goods and services and direct taxation changes, based as they are on the particular definitions of government outlays and taxation that are used in their simulations. The EEC simulations – based on a group of countries comparable to some extent to that for which the OECD simulations were undertaken – suggest that there are some combinations of direct tax changes that would have a bigger effect, and others that would have less effect, on output and employment or unemployment than changes in public investment or public consumption for the same effect on the fiscal balance.

Similarly, the McKibbin simulations for the US imply that both government expenditures on infrastructure and other government outlays, considered generally, have a greater effect than a labour tax credit (which would be somewhat analogous to a cut in employers' social security contributions in Europe), but less than some other types of tax change, including an investment tax credit.

Simulations with different models for a number of countries, reported in Chan-Lee and Kato (1984) also suggested that in every case the effect on output and employment of changes in non-wage government expenditures was greater than those of income tax cuts for a given initial effect on the fiscal balance. On the other hand, some results reported by Knoester (1988) suggest the opposite conclusion as being the more likely – though he appears to be simulating a wider range of government expenditures than non-wage expenditure alone. But an OECD simulation for the seven major countries in the mid-1980s suggested that, over five years, a cut in personal income tax had rather more effect on real GDP than an equivalent change in government non-wage expenditure.

On a priori grounds one might perhaps expect that, initially, government expenditures on goods and services would have the greater effect on output and employment, and that when the recipients of increased disposable income resulting from tax cuts increased their spending, this might be mainly a year or two later.

That pattern seems to be confirmed by the simulations for government expenditure and income tax cuts in the seven major OECD countries by the OECD in the mid-1980s. The main effect of a rise in government non-wage expenditure upon real GDP or employment (especially for a given change in the government deficit in each year) is clearly felt in the first two years or three years, whereas the effect on real GDP of the income tax cuts is spread much more evenly over the five years of the simulation, and is generally smaller in the first year than in most subsequent years.

This means that comparisons between the relative effects of these two fiscal instruments can give different results according to the number of years covered in the results of the simulations. The results for a number of countries, with the various models for those individual countries, reported in Chan-Lee and Kato (1984), also indicate that income tax cuts take a year or two before working up to their maximum effect (for every country covered); whereas for changes in government expenditure the maximum effect on real GDP is in four cases in the first year and in four other cases in the second year. This evidence therefore tends to confirm the a priori reasoning that government outlays (or, at any rate, those on goods and services, if not those on transfers) affect GDP almost at once, whereas tax changes have their effect only with a longer lag; but that this a priori reasoning tells us nothing about which of the two has the greater effect over a period of years.

But, taken as a whole, this evidence implies that there are likely to be one or more types of tax cut that have less effect on real output or employment over a period of several years than at least some types of government outlays, for a given effect on the budget balance. This means that different combinations of taxation and outlays can provide a stimulus with either a rise or a fall in the budget deficit (or surplus), or, indeed, with no change in it.

Knoester (1995) simulates an annual cut of 1% per annum on public spending for the US and an equal simultaneous cut in direct taxation plus social security contributions. His results indicate that this would give a net stimulus to the volume of production, small in the first year but substantial by the fifth year. In other words, he finds that a change in the general level of public spending in the US has less effect on output than does an equivalent cut in direct taxation. This result is not easy to reconcile with an earlier simulation by Knoester (1988), in which the effect on real GDP of a rise in public spending in the US appears to be about twice as great as that of a change of the same size in direct taxation. But the McKibbin and Bagnoli simulations (in Table 8.5) suggest that different forms of government outlay have very different effects on real GDP; and (coupled with Knoester's simulations) suggest that different patterns of change in direct taxation appear likely to have substantially different effects.

A conclusion that would be consistent with all the results would be that public sector expenditure on wage items had a greater effect on real GDP than that on non-wage items.

Effects on Employment and Unemployment

The relative effects of the different fiscal instruments upon employment or unemployment are similar to those on real output.

As might be expected, however, public sector employment expenditure ranks at the top in terms of its effects on employment. (This suggests that if a government tries to reduce the budget deficit by cuts in its employment, especially strong counter-acting measures from other arms of macroeconomic policy will be required if a general rise in unemployment is to be avoided.)

Perhaps surprisingly, cuts in indirect taxation have a much stronger effect on employment than on real output, ranking above other types of tax cut simulated. (Again, this means that attempts to reduce a budget deficit by increasing indirect taxation are especially likely to reduce employment.)

The effect on employment – as on real GDP – of cuts in corporation taxation as indicated in the table for the US is very much less than the effects in the other simulations either for personal income tax cuts, or for cuts in direct taxation generally.

Effects on Inflation

The upward pressure on inflation for a given stimulus to real GDP when income tax is cut, appears in the various sets of figures to be less than that which results from non-wage government expenditure. But a cut in direct taxation in general (including social security or national insurance contributions) increases inflation by less for a given stimulus to real GDP than cuts in personal income tax alone, and still less than government expenditure generally. If the effects of cuts in indirect taxation are added, clearly the cutting of taxation in general becomes less inflationary (and more likely to reduce inflation over the five years) if indirect taxes are the main ones that are cut than if direct taxation alone is cut. If, therefore, the proportionate extent to which indirect taxation is cut is reasonably large, a general cut in total taxation may be expected to have a downward effect on inflation over the five-year period, or at any rate less upward effect than government expenditure. In the only result among those included in Table 8.2 for major OECD countries where a cut in direct taxation has a greater upward effect on inflation than does a rise in public spending (Canada), a small cut in indirect taxation occurring at the same time would reduce the upward pressure of the total tax cut on inflation below that of government spending for a given stimulus to real GDP.

The results from the various models discussed above are consistent with those for the EEC (in the mid-1980s) – the other large area for which indicators of effects of a range of fiscal measures on all these macroeconomic objectives are available. (See Table 8.6.) In both cases government outlays are more inflationary than some or all of the tax cuts simulated for a given stimulus to real GDP for a given rise in the budget deficit; except that it is uncertain for the simulations for the US whether income tax cuts are more or less inflationary than government outlays, in view of their concentration on higher income groups in the McKibbin and Bagnoli simulation and conflicting conclusions on this point from the other simulations. But the fact that both indirect tax cuts and cuts in employers' social security contributions have a downward effect on inflation in the EEC means that combinations of cuts in indirect and direct taxation together could readily be found that would reduce inflation, whereas government expenditure would increase it.

The simulations for the UK may also be interpreted as suggesting, on balance, that government outlays are likely to be more inflationary than one or more of the types of tax cuts simulated – probably more inflationary over the five-year period than income tax cuts in the form simulated (a cut in the standard rate), and certainly more so than cuts in VAT, which in several of the models have a downward effect on inflation.

Effects on Net Wealth

The main conclusion about the relative effects of the various fiscal instruments on net wealth is that government investment expenditure is likely to have a positive effect, but that government spending generally is likely to reduce net wealth more than income tax cuts – which may in some countries increase net wealth. Investment tax credits, corporation tax cuts and perhaps cuts in employers' social security contributions may have an upward effect on net wealth (or at least have less downward effect on it than government consumption or cuts in income tax or in indirect taxation).

The table showing the relative ranking in terms of the effects of different fiscal instruments on net wealth for a given effect on the budget balance (at the end of Chapter 6) shows that public infrastructure investment, investment tax credits, cuts in employers' social security contributions and corporation tax cuts ranked above indirect tax cuts, personal income tax cuts and government consumption.

The widely varying effects of different instruments upon net wealth mean that there is no presumption that a movement of the budget balance towards surplus will increase net wealth (or 'national saving'), or strengthen the current account balance (one of the two constituents of net wealth). A reduction in the budget deficit taking the form of a cut in government investment is most likely to reduce net wealth; and a movement in a contractionary direction of one or more of the instruments near the top of the list, coupled with a somewhat smaller contractionary movement of one of those near the bottom of the list would move the budget towards surplus while presumably reducing net wealth ('saving').

CONCLUSIONS

The conclusions to be drawn from the various simulations discussed in earlier sections of this chapter therefore imply that attempts to cut the budget deficit by raising indirect taxation, or perhaps by increases in taxes on labour (employers' social security contributions in continental Europe or employers' national insurance contributions in the UK), or a reduction in labour tax credits in the US, would generally have the worst effects on macroeconomic objectives in terms of inflation, output and employment for a given change in real GDP.

Both cuts in indirect taxation and cuts in taxes on labour appear, on the available evidence, to have the best effects by way of stimulating output or employment while tending to reduce inflation over a period of at least five years. In addition, cuts in taxes on labour appear to have an upward effect on net wealth, the stimulus that they give to private investment exceeding the tendency of cuts in these taxes to weaken the current account of the balance of payments for the EEC, and the trade balance in the simulation for the US.

Generally speaking, cuts in personal income taxation are likely to have a smaller downward (or even an upward) effect on net wealth – at least in relation to their effect on real GDP – than do increases in government consumption. But increases in government infrastructure investment or a rise in a permanent investment tax credit could be expected to increase net wealth appreciably.

In short, there are a wide variety of fiscal instruments that have widely varying effects on different objectives. This means that there are usually ways of *reducing* a budget deficit that will have helpful effects on one or more of these objectives, whereas with other combinations of these instruments there will be ways of *increasing* the budget deficit that will have helpful effects.

Emphasis upon the effect of fiscal policy on the budget balance does not, therefore, contribute to a useful discussion of macroeconomic policy.

Table 8.15: Approximate ranking of various fiscal instruments in order of their effects on different macroeconomic objectives over a five-year period
(As shown in tables at the end of Chapters 3, 4, 5 and 6)

	Output	Employment	Prices & Inflation	Net wealth
Government outlays:				
Government employment expenditure	1	1	11	9
Government investment expenditure	2	4	7	1
Government non-wage expenditure	8	11	10	8
Government consumption	9	8	8	10
Social security transfers	10	9	9	11
Tax cuts or credits:				
Investment tax credit	3	6	4	2
Labour tax credit	4	5	3	5
Cut in VAT	5	2	1	7
Cut in company or corporation tax	7	7	5	4
Cut in employers' social security or national insurance contributions	6	3	2	3
Personal income tax cuts	11	10	6	6

Notes:
1 A low figure signifies the greatest effect in increasing real output, employment or net wealth, or in minimising or reducing inflation and unemployment, when the instrument is moved in an expansionary direction. The precise ranking is to some extent impressionistic, as the results of the various simulations differ somewhat in the rankings. One should not, in any event, expect the ranking to be identical from one country or group of countries to another.
2 Some of the categories of government expenditure are to some extent overlapping.
3 The effects of the various instruments on the different objectives is assumed to be symmetrical, none of the simulations drawn upon having produced evidence to the contrary.

If the aim is to provide a real stimulus without increasing the budget deficit, one of the measures near the top of the table should be changed in an expansionary direction, and any undesired effect on the budget balance offset by a contractionary movement of one of the measures near the bottom of the table. For instance, a rise in government investment expenditure or a cut in value-added tax might be combined with a reduction in government consumption or non-wage expenditure, or a rise in personal income tax.

If the aim is to reduce the budget deficit without reducing real output or increasing inflation, the appropriate combination of measures would involve combining a contractionary movement of one of the measures nearer to the bottom of the table with a movement of one of the measures near the top of the table in an expansionary direction.

An example of such a combination might be a cut in value-added tax combined with a rise in income tax or a reduction in government consumption expenditures. Some combinations of measures that would reduce the budget deficit while both holding down inflation and holding up real output will be considered in the final chapter.

9 Policy Conclusions

Earlier chapters have argued that it is not helpful to look upon changes in the budget balance as indicators of the macroeconomic effects of fiscal policy changes, mainly because different outlays and revenues may have different effects on important macroeconomic targets for the same effect on the budget balance.

This is not to deny that a rise in government borrowing – that is, a rise in its deficit – has certain social costs. These arise mainly out of the taxation that will need to be raised in future in order to service the debt. As an alternative means of financing a higher debt, a government may be tempted by a high level of debt to tolerate a higher rate of inflation in order to 'service' its debts by inflicting on its creditors (so far as it is able to do so) the costs associated with servicing the debt. A higher level of government borrowing may also crowd out useful forms of private investment. Awareness of these and other possible future costs is the reasonable basis for the widespread antipathy towards the running of higher deficits and to increasing the size of the country's national debt (that is, the debt owed by its government).

Many of these effects of running a budget deficit consist of the damage done to output or to consumer satisfaction by the extra taxes that will need to be raised in future to service a higher level of government debt – for it is virtually impossible to find any taxes that will not have any such effects. Moreover, most forms of government outlay have some good effects, so that reducing them will to that extent have adverse social effects.

Certainly, if the level of debt could be reduced at a stroke and without any change in government outlays or taxation, reducing the budget deficit could be a valid aim in itself. But reducing a budget deficit inevitably involves either some rise in taxation or some cut in government spending, either or both of which will normally involve certain social costs, which have therefore to be set against whatever social benefit is expected to result from a reduction in government borrowing. It is the failure to take these costs into account that leads to superficial analysis of the effects of reducing the level of government borrowing; for it is reasonable to suggest reducing the budget deficit only in the context of whatever rises in taxation or decreases in government spending are proposed to bring about that fall in government borrowing.

This also means that there will presumably always be some ways of reducing a budget deficit that would have a more adverse effect on social welfare than some combinations of measures that would allow the deficit to rise. This is the basic reason why targeting the budget deficit is dangerous to social and economic welfare.

Any assessment of the net effect of these changes thus needs to take account of whatever social benefits are expected to result from the reduction of government borrowing in itself, together with whatever social costs will be inflicted by the higher taxation or reductions in government outlays that are needed to effect the decline in government borrowing.

This is not to deny that some forms of government outlay are wasteful, and that the resources employed in those ways would be better employed elsewhere. But, where that is so, the economies in government spending should be made in any event – quite apart from any effect on the budget balance – and the resources so released made available to the private sector by appropriate forms of tax cut, so that there is no presumption that there will be any effect in either direction in the budget deficit when those changes in fiscal policy have been made. (It is equally true that the private sector may also waste resources – which could be better employed in the public sector.)

The principal analysis in this book has been of the *macroeconomic* effects of alternative ways of changing the budget balance. The social costs of any effects on the pattern of consumption or production, or on the distribution of income, should, however, also be considered, in addition to any social costs and benefits of whatever effect they may have on the budget balance.

Earlier chapters have stressed that different ways of changing the budget balance by a given amount may have widely varying macroeconomic effects – not only in size, but sometimes even in direction. If it were generally true that effecting a given change in the budget balance by a cut in government spending was likely to have better macroeconomic effects than rises in taxation, it would be a simple matter to add to any prescription for cutting the budget deficit the additional policy prescription that this should be done by a reduction on the outlay side. But – to judge from the various simulations drawn upon in earlier chapters (as well as a priori reasoning) – there are always some forms of *cut* in government spending that will have adverse macroeconomic (and other social) effects sufficient to equal or exceed whatever net social benefits are expected to result from some forms of tax increase. It is therefore important not to make superficial policy prescriptions to the effect that the level of government borrowing should be reduced by economies on the outlay side (or, for that matter, by increases in taxation).

Simple generalisations to the effect that government outlays are generally likely to be more inflationary than tax cuts, for example, are not likely to be reliable guides to policy. Such statements may be true for particular countries, and for particular patterns of outlays and revenue that may prevail in a particular period. But as different government outlays and different types of taxation are likely to have different effects from one another on inflation (or on any other macroeconomic target), it is likely to be more useful to consider the probable relative effects on macroeconomic policy objectives of changes in the *pattern* of government outlays or that of government revenues. Indeed, so long as any given revenue change has different macroeconomic effects from some other revenue change, or from some form of government outlay having the same effect on the budget balance, it must be true that it is not possible to assert with confidence either the size or the direction of the effect on any given macro objective of a given change in the budget balance.

Other chapters have discussed some of the reasons to believe that the effects of different government outlays may differ from one another; and reasons to believe that different types of taxation may have different effects on macro objectives for the same effect on the budget balance. The present chapter draws these threads together, to discuss some evidence about the relative effects of both different types of taxation and of different types of government outlay (for a given effect on the budget balance).

The main conclusion from the foregoing chapters is in one sense a negative one: namely, that discussion of the budget deficit (or the PSBR in Britain) – its level and changes in it – is not a helpful guide to wise macroeconomic policy decisions.

The only objective of policy for which the budget balance (and thus changes in the government's indebtedness) is an appropriate target, is the narrow one of affecting the amount of interest that the government has to pay (and even this depends not only on the budget balance but the means chosen to finance it).

But that objective makes no more sense as a single policy objective than for a business to consider only the costs of borrowing without taking account of the use to which it could put the borrowed funds. There is no point in borrowing unless the view is taken that the benefits to be derived from making use of the borrowed funds exceed the cost of the borrowing. That is true for a country, a government, a firm or an individual.

EXPANSIONARY FISCAL POLICIES WITHOUT BUDGET DEFICITS

We have seen in earlier chapters that if different fiscal measures having the same effect on the budget balance have different effects on the level of real output or employment, it is not necessarily true that a more expansionary fiscal policy will involve moving the budget balance in the direction of (a higher) deficit.

To take a very simple example, suppose that there is a tax increase that applies largely to higher income groups, and a reduction in taxes (or rise in transfer payments) that affects mainly lower-income groups, but on a scale that leaves the budget balance slightly more in surplus (or less in deficit) than before the change of policy. One would expect that these two changes together would provide some stimulus to demand, and thus to real output and employment. For it is highly probable that the lower-income groups will spend an appreciably greater sum out of their additional disposable incomes than the reduction in spending that will result on the part of the people in higher income groups when the taxes they pay are increased. It is certainly possible that in such a case there will be a net stimulus to demand, even if the budget balance changes somewhat in the direction of surplus.

To take another example, suppose that the government increases taxation by slightly more than a simultaneous rise in its expenditure on goods and services. It is quite possible that in such a case a move of the budget balance towards surplus will lead to some net stimulus to demand, at least in the short run, as the government expenditure enters immediately into the income stream, creating demand for goods and services, whereas the reduction in disposable income brought about by the rise in taxation will not affect expenditure unless and until people reduce their spending as a consequence of having to pay higher taxes. There is no general presumption, therefore, that a fiscal stimulus requires a net movement of the budget balance in the direction of deficit.

A similar conclusion arises if there is a shift in the pattern of taxation away from those types of tax that have a relatively large effect in reducing expenditure, towards those types of taxation that do not reduce private spending to the same extent. One reason that this may occur is that, as we have seen in earlier chapters, some forms of taxation tend to increase costs and the price level to a greater extent than others – whereas other types of taxation tend to reduce any upward pressure on prices. This means that a shift from the more inflationary types of taxation towards those that are less inflationary will tend to have a net upward effect on real demand (for a given upward effect on nominal demand). Even if this shift of taxation was on a scale that slightly increased tax proceeds (whether in nominal or real terms), the resulting movement of the budget balance in the direction of surplus could still bring about an increase in activity.

By a similar argument, it is obviously possible to provide a net stimulus to activity while keeping the budget balance unchanged (whether in real or nominal terms) – provided only that there are some forms of outlay or taxation that will have different effects from others upon real output or employment for a given effect on the budget balance.

This leads to the important, but widely neglected, conclusion that it is highly misleading to identify the provision of a fiscal stimulus with a movement of the budget balance in the direction of deficit. This is clearly relevant to the (highly questionable) argument that is sometimes raised to the effect that the provision of a fiscal stimulus – usually assumed to mean a rise in government debt levels – may not stimulate expenditure, as individuals will take account (on this view) of the additional taxation to which they and their heirs will be subjected as a result of the rise in national debt. It is not even necessary to raise the reasonable objection to this argument that people do not in fact think in this way – either for themselves or their heirs – if the provision of a fiscal stimulus is not necessarily to be identified with a rise in the level of the national debt. If, however, people did in fact react to the rise in the level of the national debt by reducing their expenditure (for a given level of disposable income) to a fully offsetting extent, there would be an argument for the provision of more of the stimulus by changes in the *pattern* of outlays and revenue, and less (or none) of it by increases in the level of the budget deficit.

In fact, as the results of simulations reported in earlier chapters have shown, all the types of fiscal stimulus tested (considered individually) do appear to have a positive effect on real output and employment over the short and medium term (up to at least five years); and for the most part they have different relative effects for a given change in the budget balance. For example, the most recent simulations undertaken by the University of Warwick Macroeconomic Modelling Bureau with various models of the UK economy of various types of fiscal stimulus all suggest a net increase in real GDP over at least the average of the first five years after the change (as well as also, in most cases, for each of the first five years individually); and all but one of them suggest that they will bring about a fall in unemployment over the same period.

It may also be observed that the most recent simulations available with some of these models suggest that the level of public sector borrowing may even be reduced by *cuts* in income tax, and – less clearly – perhaps even by increases in government outlays. For it is possible for output, incomes and employment to be stimulated by certain types of fiscal expansion to such an extent that the level of government borrowing falls, as tax receipts rise and outlays on unemployment benefits fall as a result of the tax cuts or rises in government expenditure. So far as this might be true, it would add another argument for the view that expansionary fiscal measures do not necessarily involve a movement of the budget balance in the direction of deficit.

THE BUDGET DEFICIT AS A 'CONSTRAINT' ON GOVERNMENTS

The strongest argument that may be raised by those advocating the use of the level of the budget deficit as an intermediate target of policy, is that it may impose a desirable constraint on governments that are inclined to make irresponsible fiscal decisions. Governments have often imposed such targets on themselves, in the hope of convincing the electorate or the financial markets of their fiscal rectitude. The IMF frequently includes such targets in the programmes that it agrees with the governments of countries that are making large drawings on the Fund: while the OECD often tells member countries to reduce their budget deficits.

The adoption of such targets *may* happen to have the desired effect on governments, and this *may* tend to increase economic welfare. But they may equally well lead governments to take unwise decisions. Certainly, the net fiscal balance is a simpler intermediate target than ones incorporating suggestions about what combination of changes in outlays and revenue would be in the country's best interests; and, as such, budget deficit targets may be thought more likely to be understood and implemented by politicians. There may even be cases where *any* form of reduction in the fiscal deficit – almost irrespective of the measures whereby this is achieved – may be advantageous. But the cases where that is true are most likely to be where the country in question starts from a very high rate of inflation, and where increases in the fiscal deficit are likely to be financed by the creation of central bank credit. Even in those cases, however, there will always be better and worse ways of effecting a given reduction in the fiscal deficit (and almost always some ways of doing this that will bring a net social cost).

But certainly in developed countries, where inflation is now low and where resort to the central bank to finance a deficit is much less likely to occur, it is always appropriate to consider what combinations of measures to reduce the deficit (or, indeed, to increase it) will tend, on balance, to increase economic welfare; and which will not. For there will always be some combinations of measures available to cut the deficit that will have worse effects on welfare (by reducing employment and output, or by bringing about an inferior allocation of resources) than whatever favourable effects are expected to follow from the reduction of the national debt and the interest upon it resulting from the cut in the fiscal deficit.

This means that the imposition of a budget deficit constraint in such countries must be assumed to be potentially welfare-reducing if implemented in some ways, even if it can be expected to be welfare-increasing if it is carried out in others. The 'constraint' on governments imposed by this intermediate target may therefore turn out to be a constraint against the implementation of *good* policies, and not necessarily a constraint against the adoption of *bad* ones. Indeed, there is no necessary presumption that it is more likely to induce good policies than bad ones.

It is said that one argument for using the budget balance as a target is that the imposition by the IMF (for example) of more detailed targets for spending or taxation may be unacceptable politically to governments that are making drawings on the IMF – though targets for some types of spending are now often included in the conditions imposed by the IMF. On the other hand, some governments welcome such more detailed targets, as making it politically easier for them to implement policies that they know to be necessary. If the IMF specifies a target purely in terms of the budget balance, this may also lead the government concerned to push certain outlays 'off-budget'; though, provided that they remain within the public sector, the imposition of a public sector borrowing requirement, rather than a budget deficit target, should make this much more difficult, or even impossible.*

THE VIEW THAT FISCAL MEASURES ARE INEFFECTIVE

It is not surprising, in view of the above arguments and the evidence of earlier chapters, that when writers have tried to assess the effects of changes in budget balances they have come up with widely varying and often inconclusive results. This is exactly what one would expect.

But when their inconclusive results are used to throw doubt upon whether expansionary fiscal policy (by which they mean a bigger budget deficit) is ineffective, that is an indefensible conclusion, relying as it does on the tacit assumption that a fiscal stimulus must be one that moves the budget balance in the direction of deficit.

As we have seen, however, if both the outlay side and the taxation side can be changed, as well as the mix of taxes or the mix of government outlays, there is no reason why expansionary fiscal measures should not be effective in working towards the various macroeconomic objectives – even though changes in the budget balance (in itself) are not found to have a discernible and reliable effect on those objectives. The essential requirement is that the individual items in the budget – or, at the very least, some of the principal categories – should be assessed in relation to their respective ability to affect the different macroeconomic objectives. If this is done, an appropriate combination of them can then be chosen to provide a net stimulus, irrespective

---

* In drafting this section I have benefited greatly from discussions with Max Corden, Graeme Dorrance and Jocelyn Horne.

of its effect on the budget balance – which is thus simply the residual result
of the decisions made about both sides of the budget.

The various simulations that have been drawn upon in earlier chapters
suggest certain general conclusions for policy.

In the first place, they all suggest that, over the period of five (or in some
cases seven) years to which they apply, fiscal measures have appreciable effects
upon real output, employment and inflation – and probably also on the
current account balance and the level of investment relative to total output
(though the evidence of this is much less extensive). They thus give no support
to anyone who still believes that individual fiscal measures have a negligible
effect on the macroeconomic target variables over the short or medium run.
(This is despite the fact that many of the models have built into them some
sort of forward-looking expectations that in effect often make the simulated
long-run effects of policy changes negligible.)

Secondly, there are different degrees of effect on real output, employment
and inflation for (all or nearly all of) the different fiscal measures simulated.
From this follows the important conclusion that there are changes in the
composition of taxation and outlays that can stimulate output or employment,
and affect the rate of inflation, but which do not have the effect of also raising
the budget deficit. The almost automatic identification in many people's minds
of a bigger deficit with expansionary fiscal policies is thus seen to be
thoroughly misleading; for some expansionary policies will involve a bigger
deficit, some no change in the deficit, and some a move towards surplus.

It is true that the evidence is mixed as to which types of fiscal measures
have the greatest effect on any given macroeconomic target for a given
effect on the budget balance, and that more reliable models are probably needed
to give greater guidance. But, in any case, decisions need to be taken in the
light of the best available estimates of the relative effects of the different
available fiscal measures on the main macroeconomic objectives before
wise decisions can be made about what fiscal measures should be changed.

Certain general conclusions about the ranking of the different instruments
can be drawn (with varying degrees of confidence) on the basis of the results
available for a number of different models, and for several different countries
(though one should not expect identical conclusions on these matters to
apply to all simulations or to all countries).

One result of comparing these various simulations is that there is no clear
conclusion between the ranking of government outlays in general compared
with taxation in general. This is partly because different simulations test
different types of tax change and different types of government expenditure,
and the effects differ between one form of outlay and another, and also as
between one type of tax change and another. The most recent available

simulation with the OECD's Interlink model provides evidence that changes in *non-wage* government outlays have a smaller effect on output or employment than a change in the total of a range of direct taxes, and that they are also more inflationary than cuts in those direct taxes for a given change in government borrowing over the whole period .

But there is evidence from a number of other simulations (including those with UK models, and those with models from a number of other countries) that government expenditure generally, or government employment expenditure, have a greater effect on output or employment, especially over two or three years, than income tax changes (taken alone, rather than as part of a package of direct taxation measures) for a given effect on the budget deficit (especially in relation to the change in the budget balance during the initial year).

The evidence is also mixed as to whether cuts in indirect taxation or in taxes on employment (employers' national insurance contributions in Britain and social security payments in continental Europe) are more or less expansionary than cuts in income tax for a given effect on the budget balance. But a simulation for the EEC (as it was in the early to mid-1980s) suggested that government outlays on public investment were more expansionary in terms of their effect on real GDP than income tax cuts; but that cuts in indirect tax and in employers' social security contributions were both more expansionary than public investment or cuts in household income tax. Clearly, disaggregation of government outlays (perhaps into investment, consumption and social security transfers, as well as into wage and non-wage expenditures) is desirable, as well as simulations of a wide range of different types of tax change. As evidence of the relative effects of these various types of fiscal instrument upon real output and employment is accumulated, it will be possible to say with greater confidence what combination of measures will provide a stimulus without increasing the budget deficit – if this is considered to be one desirable aim of policy.

There is more that can be said with confidence about the relative effects of different fiscal instruments on inflation. The simulations of *cuts* in indirect taxes and in employers' social security or national insurance contributions, suggest that those measures, especially cuts in indirect taxation, will result in *downward* pressure on prices over the five-year period covered in most of the simulations (or, at worst, after a few years, less upward pressure on inflation than income tax cuts); but that cuts in income tax and (generally to a greater extent) increases in at least some forms of government outlays will make inflation worse in the immediately succeeding years.

If, therefore, the criterion is to provide a stimulus with minimal upward effect on inflation – or even while reducing inflation at the same time – there seem to be instruments (cuts in indirect taxation and taxes on employment – such as employers' social security contributions) that are likely (even taken alone) to have this effect over both the short term and the medium term Moreover, even if cuts in indirect taxation or in employers' social security contributions do not actually exert a downward impact on prices, providing only that they exert less upward pressure on prices than do income tax cuts or rises in some types of government outlays, a non-inflationary stimulus is possible, often in combination with a reduced budget deficit. For, if that is so, a shift from indirect taxation and from employers' social security contributions towards direct taxation or economies in government outlays could, in those cases, provide a stimulus while still reducing inflation.

But the EEC simulation also suggests that if one compares government consumption or investment outlays with income tax cuts, the two criteria – minimising the upward effect on the budget deficit, and minimising the upward effect on inflation for a given real stimulus – would be in conflict, as the cut in income tax appears on these simulations to have the smaller upward effect on inflation of these two measures; whereas if income tax cuts are used to provide a given stimulus to real GDP, a greater rise in the budget deficit would be required than if the same stimulus were provided by government consumption or investment.

By the same token, this means that attempts to reduce the budget deficit by way of higher levels of indirect taxation or higher taxation on employment would be misguided, in the sense that they will have a bigger downward effect on output or employment, and less (if any) downward effect on inflation over the medium term than will increases in income tax or cuts in some forms of government outlay having the same effect on the budget balance.

The evidence on whether a shift away from indirect towards direct taxation would have an upward effect on national wealth – productive investment less changes in external net assets or liabilities – is not clear cut, though evidence for the US suggests that this would be true in that country (see Chapter 8). Probably one can say, on the basis of the evidence considered in earlier chapters, that there is at any rate no good reason on these grounds to negate the policy prescription that is directed towards providing any desired stimulus with minimal upward effect on inflation. In several cases, some types of government outlay, though not government investment expenditures, have a greater downward effect on net wealth than cuts in indirect taxation.

Evidence from various simulations and a priori arguments have been adduced in Chapter 5 to show that the rate of inflation in a particular year is likely to be influenced by the particular combination of fiscal measures chosen – even at a given budget deficit or surplus. The setting of monetary policy appears also to play a part in affecting the rate of inflation at any given level of employment or of real output relative to capacity; and it may in some cases have a bearing upon the ranking of different fiscal measures in terms of their effects on certain other macroeconomic objectives, though generally it will alter their relative effect, rather than their ranking.

This being so, it makes no sense to hold the level of unemployment above that which would otherwise have been chosen, if the purpose of doing so is merely to reduce the rate of inflation over, say a three to five-year period.

That alleged benefit is often claimed for recessions. But if there are other ways of achieving the same aim, it is not logical to credit the recession with holding down inflation. If the effects of an expansionary fiscal policy on the budget deficit are adduced as an argument for refraining from taking expansionary fiscal action, and so permitting a recession to continue, this is not in fact a valid argument if changes in the *make-up* of the budget at a given level of the budget balance can stimulate activity and reduce inflation.

For we have seen how various changes in the fiscal mix can reduce inflation without reducing output or employment. In any event, some would argue that any downward effect that a rise in unemployment may have on inflation (given the setting of fiscal instruments and monetary policy) will be only temporary, and inflation will then return to whatever rate the other influences at work may determine.

If the budget deficit or PSBR has to be accepted as, to some extent, an object of policy in itself – if only because markets think it should be – then the particular combination of measures with which that budgetary target is achieved will affect the rate of inflation at any given level of employment or economic activity in immediately succeeding years. It is true that if the budget balance is not thought to be a constraint on policy in itself, the range of combinations of different fiscal instruments available will be larger; but even if it has to be accepted as one object of policy, there will clearly be better and worse ways of achieving it from the point of view of achieving the basic macroeconomic targets of high employment, low inflation, and an adequate but not excessive emphasis on investment compared with consumption.

'Balancing the Budget'

An extreme form of 'budget deficit targeting' is that of balancing the budget. There is no general presumption that a government should balance its budget (in any given year or period, or on any one of innumerable possible definitions) – any more than there is a presumption that a business or a family should never borrow. In particular, the burden of the financing of capital outlays may defensibly be shared between the present generation and future generations, by imposing on the future generations some of the taxation needed to service the debt that finances the capital investments from which they will benefit. 'Capital investment' may reasonably be defined to include investment in human capital, and thus some part of a country's investment in education and health.

When people make it their aim to balance the budget – starting from a situation of budget deficit – they presumably mean that in their view too high a proportion of the servicing costs is being imposed on posterity. But if this is so, there is no presumption that every possible manner of bringing the budget into balance will solve this problem. If the tax burden that is being imposed on posterity by present levels of government borrowing is excessive, presumably some period of budget surpluses would be needed to reduce the present burden imposed on posterity. But, in any case, the closer the present level of government debt and the budget balance are to what is optimal, the greater the risk that the social costs of increasing taxation or reducing government outlays will exceed whatever social benefits are thought likely to result from a reduction in government borrowing.

It is, in any case, presumably always true that there will be some ways of reducing government outlays or increasing taxation that will inflict greater social costs on the community than the social benefits that are expected to arise from reducing the level of government borrowing by increasing taxation or reducing government outlays. One obvious way is as a result of cutting government spending on productive investment (whether in material or human capital), or a rise in taxation imposed upon useful productive investment (directly, or indirectly through corporation tax or payroll taxes, for example). Those ways of trying to increase net saving will almost certainly impose additional burdens on posterity, rather than alleviate those burdens.

Furthermore, as there are many different defensible definitions of what constitutes budget balance, there is no particular reason to expect that balance on one particular definition will bring the maximum of social benefit. If government capital outlays are not distinguished from current outlays – as appears to be true of figures generally quoted in relation to the US – this is likely to result in an insufficient level of public investment, and an inadequate level of government borrowing to finance it, if budget balance (thus defined) is made a target.

There are in any case many defensible definitions of the budget deficit; and this means that there can be a reduction in the deficit on one definition at the same time as it is being increased on some other – equally or more defensible – definition.

A particular reason for caution in advocating reductions in the budget deficit as being in the interests of posterity, is that many ways of reducing the budget deficit will not only reduce the level of useful productive investment (private or public, or both), whether in human or material capital, but will often also reduce real output over some considerable period. So far as that occurs, it means that posterity will have less resources available to finance whatever level of national debt has to be serviced. This must be set against the reduction in the level of debt servicing that may be brought about by the reduction in the level of the national debt when a budget deficit is cut. It is thus quite possible for the burden of debt imposed on posterity to be increased by measures to reduce the budget deficit if those measures bring about a reduction in the level of output and investment available to posterity.

Does the Direction of the Macro Effects of a Budget Depend Partly on Whether Both Sides of it Are Being Moved in the Same Direction?

We have seen in earlier chapters that a movement away from deficit and towards surplus may sometimes be expansionary and sometimes contractionary in terms of its effects on output or employment. The cases where we found that a movement towards deficit might be contractionary were cases where some types of both taxes and government spending were cut, but one side of the budget was cut rather more than the other, or where both taxation and government outlays were increased but one side of the budget was increased by less than the other.

Either of these two cases might, as we have seen, cause a movement towards deficit to be contractionary (or, in the opposite case, a movement towards surplus to be expansionary), depending on which of the two instruments had the greater effect on output or employment for a given effect on the budget balance.

In the various simulations drawn upon earlier, with one partial exception, we have not, however, found cases where a rise in (all) government outlays (taken alone) was contractionary or a rise in (all) taxation was expansionary. (Changes in the pattern of government outlays or in the pattern of taxation may, however, be accompanied by changes in the overall level of taxation or of government outlays in such a way that a rise in taxation could be expansionary and a cut in taxation contractionary – and the same for the outlay side.)

This implies that if a rise in the budget deficit was brought about by a simultaneous rise in (all) government outlays and fall in (all types of) taxation, this could be expected to be expansionary (and conversely when government spending was cut and taxes increased). We have, however, found a simulation for the OECD as a whole where, if monetary policy is assumed to be non-accommodating, a rise in government spending or a cut in taxation may reduce output over a three-year (but not over a five-year) period ('net crowding out'), though this did not appear to be true of the instruments simulated for individual OECD countries.

Provided that both the instruments – or, more exactly, the monetary policy accompanying them – led to net crowding out, however, movements of both of them in the direction tending to increase the deficit would, in this case, inevitably be contractionary (and vice versa). Only if one of the measures that was changed led to net crowding out, whereas the other did not, could a rise in government spending accompanied by a cut in taxation lead to a net expansionary or a net contractionary effect, depending on the relative size and direction of their respective effects on output or employment.

In general, however, it is reasonable to expect that a rise in the budget deficit that takes the form of a simultaneous rise in (all) government outlays and a cut in (all types of) taxation would have an expansionary effect, as each of the two measures would individually be working in that direction (apart from the case of net crowding out, which might occur with a non-accommodating monetary policy – at any rate for a large area such as the OECD).

It is not, however, possible to say with any degree of confidence that one could make a similar generalisation about the direction of the net effect upon other macroeconomic objectives of a movement of the budget towards deficit.

In particular, the direction of the net effect upon inflation of a rise in the budget deficit could (on the evidence we have found in earlier chapters) be downwards even if government consumption were increased, provided that indirect taxes or taxes on labour inputs such as employers' social security contributions were cut sufficiently at the same time. For, in this case, the reduction in inflation resulting from the tax cuts could exceed the increase in it attributable to government consumption spending, even though both measures were tending to increase the budget deficit.

Government consumption may be expected to reduce net wealth, but government investment expenditure could be expected generally to increase national net wealth.

In the latter case, if government investment expenditures were increased and some types of taxation reduced, net national wealth could increase, even though the budget was being moved towards (greater) deficit from both sides.

Of course, if government investment were increased at the same time as one of the taxes that tended to reduce private net wealth was being reduced, this would make it the more likely that the movement towards budget deficit would increase national wealth, even though the budget deficit was being increased from both sides. A movement of the budget towards surplus will therefore not necessarily increase net wealth (or 'national saving'), even though it means a higher level of net saving by the government.

In these cases, therefore, a rise in the budget deficit brought about by a simultaneous rise in government spending and a cut in these particular taxes could well increase net national wealth (even though both instruments were being changed in a direction tending to increase the budget deficit).

CONCLUSION

The principal argument of this book has been that the direction and size of a change in the budget balance is no indication of the direction (still less, of the scale) of the effect of the fiscal measures in question upon any of the macroeconomic objectives. Targeting the budget balance (on any one of a wide range of defensible definitions) is therefore likely to lead to misguided macroeconomic policies.

On the evidence of a number of simulations for many countries, as well as a priori reasoning, we must conclude that a given change in the budget balance can have widely varying effects – both in extent and direction – upon real output, employment or unemployment, inflation, the current account balance and 'net wealth' (the aggregate of the changes in the current account and the country's stock of productive capital) – according to the combination of changes in outlays and revenue with which it is brought about.

There may be benefits for a country's borrowers as a result of a reduction in a government's borrowing – in the shape of a lower interest rate bill for the government, and possible downward effects on borrowing costs of businesses there especially if the confidence in the country in question on the part of financial markets is enhanced by the tighter budgetary policy. But it is not possible to base a change of fiscal policy on that argument alone, for the effects of whatever changes in government outlays or tax receipts are necessary to effect a given reduction in the level of government borrowing must always be brought into the calculation before one can reach a policy conclusion.

It is also sometimes argued that business confidence may be enhanced by the introduction of a tighter budget, leading to a higher level of investment expenditure.

In any case, if any adverse effects on the country's borrowing costs or on investors' confidence were to result from a rise in the budget deficit, this would not affect the ranking of different fiscal instruments having the same effect on the budget balance. The evidence that there are differences in their ranking in terms of their effects on different macroeconomic objectives leaves open the possibility of changing the fiscal mix in such a way as to have the desired effects on the various macro objectives, and by doing so to bring social benefits to set against whatever social costs may be associated with a higher budget deficit as such.

To suggest that a reduction in government borrowing is always beneficial is thus the equivalent of saying that a family or a business should always reduce or eliminate its borrowing, whatever the use to which the borrowing would have been put.

Nor is it helpful to suggest that reducing the budget deficit by reducing government outlays is always preferable to doing so by increasing taxation. For we have found that some types of government outlay have more favourable effects than others, and some forms of tax increase are more damaging than others, in terms of their relative effects on different macroeconomic objectives.

There are even some cases where two different fiscal instruments having the same effect on the budget balance, have conflicting effects on a given macro objective – an important example being the upward effects on inflation (not only immediately but also over five or more years) that may be expected to result from increases in indirect taxation or in taxes on employment (such as social security contributions in Europe), compared with the downward effect on inflation of increases in income taxation or cuts in many forms of government outlay.

Even when different fiscal measures do not, individually, have conflicting effects on a macro objective, so long as their relative effects on macro objectives (for a given change in the budget balance) differ from one another, there will always be combinations of them that will have a favourable effect on that objective, and others that will have unfavourable effects. It is therefore totally misleading to try to use changes in the budget balance/budget deficit/public sector borrowing requirement as a guide to policy.

The pressure for governments to reduce their budget deficits appears to spring partly from a view that the present generation is inflicting excessive costs on future generations – and on itself in future years – by not saving enough, thereby devoting less saving to increasing the stock of human and material capital than would be desirable. The servicing of the extra debt thus created also means that posterity will have to accept higher tax charges than otherwise.

This pressure from business, journalists, and some politicians and academics to reduce budget deficits may well often provide a useful correction to an excessive preference for present satisfactions; an excessive preference in the sense that it may lead governments to keep taxes too low and outlays too high (borrowing the difference), thereby achieving popularity at the expense of the country's social and economic welfare.

Yet one task of a government ought to be to see that the present generation does not sacrifice too much in the interests of posterity. Future generations are likely to be richer than the present one – at least in rich countries – and, in any case, it is always worth asking: 'What has posterity done for me that I should do so much for posterity?'

It is, however, probably true that, on a global scale, it is by no means certain that future generations will be better off than we are: excessive wastage of world resources and failure to make adequate resources available to finance development in the poorer countries, may well be problems calling for public and private economies to be made in order to make possible a greater flow of public and private aid to poorer nations, and a greater use of resources in ways that will reduce damage to the environment.

But that is likely to require higher government outlays – in the form of foreign aid and in conserving the environment – and merely running smaller government deficits will not in itself contribute to those aims.

If the focus of policy is the budget balance (or the level of government borrowing or government debt), attention is diverted from the significant matters of the combinations of government outlays and taxation with which any given balance is achieved; just as by focusing on the current account of the balance of payments, attention is diverted from the more important question of the use to which the extra resources obtained by means of a current account deficit are being put (and thus from the additions to the country's stock of capital – or flow of overseas aid – that would become impossible if certain types of measures were used to reduce the current account deficit).

When the government is urged to borrow less, it is usually because this is seen as adding to the country's total saving, and thus to the resources available for real investment (or reducing overseas debt). But such an analysis (if it can reasonably be so described) neglects all the repercussions of the various ways in which a budget deficit may be reduced. Obviously, reductions in disposable incomes that will result from higher taxation or lower government spending will have repercussions on the saving undertaken by the private sector, so that the proportion of a given level of income that will be saved will not necessarily rise, and will certainly not rise to the full extent of any reduction in the budget deficit.

Perhaps more important, attempts by the public and private sector to save more, if they are not complemented by adequate measures to ensure that these additional savings are employed to make possible a higher level of real investment (or overseas aid), will not necessarily lead to a higher total level of saving; for the 'paradox of thrift' (one of the most fundamental lessons of macroeconomics) is that attempts by individuals or governments to save a higher proportion of a given income will, taken by itself, reduce the flow of incomes, and to that extent also total saving. The crucial matter is, therefore, whether any additional saving is being employed to make possible a higher level of other (presumably more useful) forms of outlay than those that would have occurred in the absence of the additional saving.

Furthermore, a decision by a government to run a smaller deficit (that is, to save more out of any given level of income) will not necessarily lead to an increase in the country's net wealth (a better description of this aim of policy than 'saving', because it incorporates the idea of the saving being devoted to the production of useful capital, or to the reduction of external debt).

We have seen in Chapter 6 that different fiscal measures having the same effect on the budget balance may have widely varying effects on the country's private net wealth, and, if the government's own investment is included in the outlay side of the budget balance, also on the stock of national net wealth. This means that some combinations of measures that reduce the budget deficit will also reduce net wealth, and others that increase the budget deficit will increase net wealth.

To sum up: the budgetary balance is important as the resultant of the various forms of outlays and taxation that make it what it is, but it is those various forms of government outlay and taxation that require to be considered each on its own merits. The social costs and benefits of reducing government borrowing as such should certainly come into the calculation of what policy is appropriate, but only in the context of the costs and benefits of whatever measures are adopted on the outlay or revenue sides to bring about a given change in that balance. Failure to adopt that approach will mean that the policy adopted is as likely to bring net social costs as net social benefits, and be less beneficial than one that gives due weight to all the costs and benefits of the various alternative changes that may be made, on either side of the budget, to bring about a given change in the budget balance.

In short, if an appropriate choice is being made among all the different fiscal instruments – taking account of the macroeconomic effects of each (as well as of their other effects) – the budget balance becomes in effect a 'fifth wheel'; that is to say, it tells us nothing about the desirable setting of fiscal policy other than what we can attribute to the changes in each of the fiscal instruments that make the budget balance whatever it is.

Appendix: Suggestions for Future Simulations

The chapters of this book have drawn upon simulations for a number of countries and country groups, all of which throw some light on the effects of changes in different fiscal measures upon different macro objectives.

But the questions asked and answered in these various simulations differ greatly from one set of simulations to another. In addition to the inevitable variations between models as a consequence of their construction, there are ways in which the questions asked by the modellers, and so the answers they give, could be made more helpful for guidance about macroeconomic policy, and for comparing results of simulations using one model with those from another.

In the first place, there are many simulations that ask only about the effects of one fiscal policy measure – usually government spending, on some definition. No use has been made of these simulations in this book, as they fail to compare the effects of different fiscal measures having the same effect on the budget balance. Some of those simulations even state that they are indications of the effects of a 'fiscal policy' change – as if the results could be expected to be the same whatever the fiscal policy measure being varied. (If that were in fact so, it would be essential to provide evidence of this.) But, as we have seen, all the models that simulate more than one fiscal policy change (having the same effect on the budget balance) indicate that the effects on the main macro objectives vary greatly between one fiscal measure and another. Instead of saying that a simulation shows the results of a 'fiscal policy' change, therefore, it is important always to specify the actual fiscal measure being simulated, and to simulate more than one of them.

In the second place, it would be helpful if more than one policy measure on the tax side and more than one on the outlay side were always to be changed in future model simulations. For we have found ample evidence to suggest that different outlays, and different tax changes, have very different effects (in size and even in direction) upon particular macroeconomic objectives for the same effect on the budget balance. This is, in any case, what one would expect on a priori grounds – though that is implicitly being ignored when people discuss macroeconomic policy in terms of changes in the budget deficit or surplus.

On the tax side, at the very least there should be distinctions drawn between indirect taxation, income taxation and taxes on labour inputs (such as payroll taxes and employers' social security or national insurance contributions). If other forms of tax changes and tax concessions can be distinguished also (as in the simulations for the US by McKibbin and Bagnoli drawn upon in this book) it would be more helpful still.

On the government outlay side, at the very least one would wish to have government outlays on investment distinguished from government consumption outlays, and also from government transfer payments to households (and perhaps also those to businesses). There also appear to be significant differences (to judge from some of the simulations drawn upon in this book) between the effects of government non-wage expenditures and those of government employment expenditures. It is thus important to have these simulated separately – and not to draw policy conclusions about government outlays in general from simulations of only non-wage or only employment expenditures.

Furthermore, in measuring the change in the budget balance, it would be helpful if there could be a greater measure of consistency in matters of measurement as between one simulation and another. There will inevitably be many differences in definition of the budget balance that is being used, but it would be most useful if the simulations could in future give results both for the initial impact on the budget balance in the year that the change is made, and then also for the effect on the budget balance in each year over the whole period for which the impact is being measured. Usually it is the effect on the budget in the initial year that receives most public attention; but if one aim is to affect the level of the national debt in relation to real output, and so the level of future debt servicing, the more appropriate indicator is the change in the budget balance over a period of years.

As to the macroeconomic objectives the effects upon which are being simulated, the minimum that one would require would be the effects upon GDP/GNP and on inflation (or the price level). It is also desirable to have an indication of the effects on the current account balance; but this should always be complemented by a simulation of the effects on private investment or (preferably) total investment, including that in the public sector.

Finally, the assumption about the setting of monetary policy being made in the simulation should be made explicit. Ideally, the simulations should be done with more than one such alternative assumption. For example, it is useful to be able to compare the effects of different fiscal instruments under the assumption of a non-accommodating monetary policy (in effect, with interest rates – real or nominal – being allowed to reflect the impact of the fiscal measures) with the results that follow if monetary policy is assumed to be 'accommodating' – that is, in effect holding interest rates (real or nominal) at the level they would have been in the absence of the fiscal measures.

References

Bogaert, H. et al. (1990), 'A disequilibrium model of the Belgian economy', *Economic Modelling*, Vol. 7 No. 4.

Beenstock, M. et al. (1994), 'A Macroeconometric Model for Israel', *Economic Modelling*, Vol. 11, No. 4.

Bradley, J. et al. (1995), 'HERMIN Ireland', *Economic Modelling* Vol. 12 No. 3, July.

Chan-Lee, J. H. and Kato, H. (1984), 'A Comparison of simulation properties of national econometric models', *OECD Economic Studies*, Spring.

Church, K. B., Mitchell, P. R., Smith, P. N. and Wallis, K. F. (1993), 'Comparative Properties of Models of the UK economy', *National Institute Economic Review*, August.

Church, K. B., Mitchell, P. R., Smith, P. N. and Wallis, K. F. (1995), 'Comparative Properties of Models of the UK economy', *National Institute Economic Review*, August.

Dramais, A. (1986), 'COMPACT – a Prototype Macroeconomic Model of the European Community and the World Economy', *European Economy*, March.

Herce, J- A. and Sosvilla-Rivero, S. (1995), 'HERMIN Spain', *Economic Modelling*, Vol. 12, No. 3.

Knoester, A. (1983), 'Stagnation and the Inverted Haavelmo Effect: Some International Evidence', *De Economist*, Vol. 131 No. 4.; also as *Netherlands Ministry of Economic Affairs Reprint* 8301.

Knoester, A. (1988), 'Economic Growth in Europe, Japan and the United States', *University of Nijmwegen Institute of Economics Research Memorandum* No. 8804.

Knoester, A. (ed.) (1993), *Taxation in the United States and Europe*, Basingstoke and London: Macmillan.

Knoester, A. (1995), 'The Inverted Haavelmo Effect and its Implications for European Economic Policy', *Research Centre for Economic Policy, Erasmus University of Rotterdam Research Memorandum* 9508.

Knoester, A. and Kolodziejak, A. (1994), 'Effects of Taxation in Economic Models: A Survey', *Economic Modelling* Vol. 9 No. 4, October; also as *Research Centre for Economic Policy, Erasmus University of Rotterdam Reprint* 9404.

Leibfritz, W., Roseveare, D. and Van den Noord, P. (1994), 'Fiscal Policy, Government Debt and Economic Performance', *OECD Economics Department Working Paper*, No.144.

McKibbin, W. and Bagnoli, P. (1993), 'Fiscal Deficit Reduction: An Evaluation of Alternatives', *Brookings Discussion Papers in International Economics* No.101, July.

Modesto, L. and Neves, P. (1995), 'HERMIN: Portugal', *Economic Modelling*, Vol. 12 No. 2, July.

Perkins, J. O. N. (1979), *The Macroeconomic Mix to Stop Stagflation*, London: Macmillan.

Perkins, J. O. N. (1982), *Unemployment, Inflation and New Macroeconomic Policy*, London: Macmillan.

Perkins, J. O. N. (1985), *The Macroeconomic Mix in the Industrialised World*, London: Macmillan.

Perkins, J. O. N. (1990), *A General Approach to Macroeconomic Policy*, London: Macmillan.

Richardson, Pete (1987), 'A Review of the Simulation Properties of the OECD's Interlink Model', *OECD Economics and Statistics Department Working Papers*, No. 47.

Richardson, P., Giotto, C. and Thurman, S. (1994), 'Macroeconomic performance and fiscal policy adjustments in the medium term: alternative medium term scenarios', *OECD Working Paper* Vol. II No. 56.

Rock, James M. (ed.) (1991), *Debt and the Twin Deficits Problem*, Mountain View, CA: Mayfield Publishing Company.

Wallis, K. F. and Whitley, J. D. (1991), 'Large-scale econometric models of national economies', *Scandinavian Journal of Economics*, Vol. 93 No. 2.

Index